THE ACADEMIC'S GUIDE
TO PUBLISHING

THE ACADEMIC'S GUIDE TO PUBLISHING

Rob Kitchin and Duncan Fuller

SAGE Publications
London ● Thousand Oaks ● New Delhi

SAGE Publications Ltd
1 Oliver's Yard
55 City Road
London EC1Y 1SP

SAGE Publications Inc.
2455 Teller Road
Thousand Oaks, California 91320

SAGE Publications India Pvt Ltd
B-42, Panchsheel Enclave
Post Box 4109
New Delhi 100 017

British Library Cataloguing in Publication data

A catalogue record for this book is available from the British Library

ISBN 1 4129 0082 1
ISBN 1 4129 0083 2 (pbk)

Library of Congress Control Number 2004099485

Typeset by M Rules
Printed on paper from sustainable resources
Printed and bound in Great Britain by
The Cromwell Press Ltd, Trowbridge, Wiltshire

Contents

Preface

This book has its genesis in three interrelated exchanges that have taken place over a number of years. First, we have had numerous discussions about our own, and colleagues' experiences of writing and editing, attending and organizing seminars, workshops and conferences, of liaising with editors and publishers, and career progression. In the main, these discussions have consisted of the swapping of notes about how things seemed to work, alongside much griping about apparent injustices and the lack of transparency of many arrangements, procedures and practices in the world of academia in general, and writing in particular.

Largely as a consequence of these discussions, our second set of conversations have concerned articulating a critical analysis of transformations in the nature and organization of higher education, the increasing pressures on researchers to be more 'productive', and the cultural and institutional politics surrounding publication. Here we have become increasingly alarmed by the recent restructuring of the higher education sector across different countries, the corporatization of many universities, the widespread adoption of business-like management practices, and the increasing pervasiveness of neo-liberal imperatives in shaping university life (see Fuller and Kitchin, 2004).

As a result of this unease, our third set of discussions have concerned how life could perhaps be made easier for students and colleagues who are caught within such transformations and pressures, but are unsure of how to successfully publicise their work, or even of the options available to them.

Together these exchanges have spurred us on to explore the 'rules' of publishing research, and the extent to which increased transparency and lucidity of the many aspects of publication might help unsettle traditional and new power relations within the higher education sector and disturb exclusionary and (self-)exploitative practices by allowing increased scrutiny and reflection on what actually goes on, and how, in publishing research.

In many respects this process of explanation grew out of a conference we organized – 'Beyond the Academy? Critical Geographies in Action', held at Northumbria University in September 2001. While focusing on the politics, ethics and practicalities that academics face in feeding into policy, engaging in activism, undertaking consultancy work, contributing to local/national debates/politics, striving to engender change in local communities, and creating critical classrooms, this conference also had a recurring concern with what one participant (Jenny Robinson) called the 'production nexus' of publishing. A particular focus here was the seemingly 'black box' nature of publishing, the unwritten 'rules' of dissemination, and the growth and pernicious nature of research accountancy schemes.

It became clear from the dialogue at this meeting that many academics felt they were becoming increasingly drawn into a variety of new 'webs' of power, where status within these 'webs' was largely defined by research outputs. A focus here became what might be termed the 'performative and politicized dance of the academic', with academics simultaneously dancing in different ways (as teacher, supervisor, mentor, administrator, committee member, chairperson, researcher, writer, editor, reviewer, adviser, examiner, manager, conference organizer, activist) to different 'tunes' set by different parties (university, students, colleagues, collaborators, contributors, publishers, committees, academic bodies, research and funding agencies, research participants) (see Fuller and Kitchin, 2004). In addition, discussion also highlighted, ironically, just how little academic analysis there has been of how modern academics have been coerced into self-disciplining and exploiting their own labor for gain, what these 'gains' might be, and/or perhaps more importantly, who ultimately benefits.

From here, we therefore began preparing training materials for use by predominantly (but not exclusively) young researchers who wanted to learn how to disseminate their research effectively and strategically. Initially these were for use within our own respective institutions or at wider postgraduate training weekends. However, this soon developed into a short Internet-based guide for students within our own discipline. The latter emanated from two 'meet the editors' sessions held at the 2002 Association of American Geographers' conference held in Los Angeles (co-organized by Lawrence Berg and Rob Kitchin). At those sessions we suggested the idea of a resource website for postgraduate and faculty designed to illustrate how the publishing process works, answer basic questions about writing and publishing geographical work, and provide a number of links to useful websites, journals and publishers. It was also envisaged that, while being a useful resource for those contributing to journals, it might be a valuable site for editors – somewhere to refer an author whose paper needs significant attention, for example – while also drawing them into a critical discussion about the politics and ethics of dissemination practices. The idea was enthusiastically endorsed by the editors of twelve journals[1] (now more than thirty) and we began the process of piecing together the content of the site.[2]

The final stage in this journey has been the development of this book, which expands significantly on the website we created, and is designed to raise awareness of issues in publication and inform regardless of specialty and stage in one's career.

Our motivation in each of these related projects has been twofold. On the one hand it has been to provide advice about publishing and presenting, two pursuits that, at best, can be challenging and confusing for those unfamiliar with their workings, and at worst can lead to fruitless self-exploitation and (academic) misery. On the other it has been to generate discussion, debate and the exchange of ideas and experiences, while also exposing the ways in which research is embedded in a complex and transforming institutional landscape saturated with 'calculative practices' (that is, how concepts such as researcher 'productivity' are measured and issues such as 'worth' and 'value' are defined) that shape researchers' work routines and publication strategies.

These two motivations have shaped the book that follows. In the main, we have sought to produce a handbook that provides a comprehensive guide to all the different ways that research can be published, making transparent their structures and practices and presenting useful advice in a form that is succinct and easily digestible. There are of course other such guides or handbooks on the market (some of which are listed in Appendix 1). However, all of the ones we are familiar with focus on one or two particular aspects of publishing and presenting. For example, there is a number of books concerned with how to write in general and for different media (for example, books, journals, popular press) or how to self-publish or undertake public presentations. Few place publication in a wider context of career development and progression, or the organization and regulation of academic life.

In no way do we seek to be overly prescriptive in our discussion, trying to detail a set of cast-iron rules that, if followed, will deliver guaranteed results. Indeed, we believe there are no sure-fire rules that will ensure successful publication. There are, however, strategies and tactics that, if adopted, will improve vastly your chances of sharing your ideas and findings with your intended audience(s). Our aim has been to set out such strategies and tactics and provide useful advice and observations. In doing so, we have attempted to tread a fine line between appearing to sanction and endorse existing neo-liberal projects such as the Research Assessment Exercise in the UK (or other research accountancy exercises elsewhere) by detailing 'successful' publication strategies, and a more pessimistic line of simply attempting to help researchers survive in such publication cultures. Rest assured, we are not attempting to transform legions of under-performing academics into an army of clones, drones and/or research accountancy fodder!

Our hope, instead, is that this guide is informative and useful, and that it helps you to publicise your research 'successfully', whatever stage in your career you are at, to a level and quality defined in large part by you (and not simply your academic paymasters). We hope it makes your academic life that little bit easier, and helps you to avoid unnecessary pitfalls in disseminating your research. We also hope it raises questions about the practices and process of publishing research and opens avenues to challenge exclusionary, exploitative and unjust tendencies wherever they are encountered.

Notes

1 *ACME, Annals of Association of American Geographers, Antipode, Area, Children's Geographies, Journal of Cultural Geographies, Ethics, Place and Environment, Gender, Place and Culture, Journal of Geography in Higher Education, Professional Geographer, Social and Cultural Geography, Society and Space.* These journals have been joined by eighteen others.
2 Geo-publishing.org (http://www.nuim.ie/nirsa/geo-pub/geo-pub.html) was launched in January 2003.

REFERENCES
Fuller, D. and Kitchin, R. (2004) 'Radical theory/critical praxis', in D. Fuller and R. Kitchin (eds), *Radical Theory, Critical Praxis: Making a Difference Beyond the Academy?* Praxis E-Press. http://www.praxis-epress.org/rtcp/contents.html, pp. 1–20.

Acknowledgements

In general we have written this book from drawing and reflecting on our own experiences and observations as researchers, authors and editors, only turning to other literatures after an initial draft was completed. We have, however, also benefited from the advice of colleagues and students and we are thankful for the contributions of Kajsa Andersson, Lawrence Berg, Mike Bradshaw, Kath Browne, Martin Dodge, Paddy Duffy, Denise Grassick, Kristal Hawkins, James Monagle, Graham Moon, Pamela Moss, Tristan Palmer, Robin Poulter, and Andrew Power. In addition, we would like to thank Robert Rojek at Sage for commissioning the book. We take full responsibility for the content.

1 PUBLISHING RESEARCH

Publication is a key aspect of research. It concerns letting other people know about your research endeavours, findings and ideas. This is its prime importance – why go through all the effort of research if nobody else can learn from it? Research, after all, is about collectively exploring, examining, challenging and advancing knowledge and understanding, building on the work of previous studies and treatises. As a consequence, those who support and fund research expect researchers to engage in such collective practice. In addition, there are obvious secondary benefits to publication that relate to strategic issues such as securing a job or promotion, gaining more research funding, building a research profile, and so on.

Successfully publishing research is, unfortunately, not an inevitable outcome of academic endeavour. Just because a project produces exciting results, or a new, groundbreaking theory, does not mean that it will automatically be communicated to the wider world, with recognition and plaudits following. Completing a project or developing an idea or theory simply represents the first phase of research. Publication is the second phase and it requires many specific skills and knowledges. Without successful dissemination no one, with the exception of close colleagues, will know about your work. It is vital then that you, as a researcher, know how different forms of publication work and possess the skills to work with and exploit these media. This book provides practical and strategic advice and information on the various means by which researchers publicise their work, and how to effectively and successfully package and present research for those media.

In today's multimedia culture, methods of publicising academic endeavours are diverse, ranging from traditional outlets such as an article in a learned journal or a research monograph, to popular media such as newspapers, radio and television, to more recent inventions such as the Internet. It can also take visual or oral means, such as a poster or presentation. As the chapters in this book detail, each form of publishing has its strengths and weaknesses and reaches different audiences. For example, the strengths of academic journals relate to their high quality, assured by peer review, the fact that institutions recognize them as the most valuable or worthy form of dissemination, and that they are read by a peer audience. The weaknesses of academic journals are their formal style, their restrictions on length and content, and that a peer audience is usually very small in number (generally fellow academics who access the journals through a university library). Books provide a broader canvas to present a theory or study, often receiving some degree of marketing, and are more likely to be seen by a wider audience. Their weaknesses relate to the time and effort taken to write them, the reliance on publishers for marketing and distribution, and their cost. Conference talks allow a work in progress to be presented to, and discussed by, peers, but time constraints often limit the content to one or two specific points and the audience is usually quite small and select. Newspapers and other forms of popular press such as magazines provide access to a very large potential audience and usually universities and colleges will welcome any coverage, but they are very restrictive in terms of content, and controlling the message presented can be difficult. And so on.

For the uninitiated, the workings of these various media can be fairly opaque. Indeed, if your experiences are the same as ours, most researchers seemingly learn how each form of publication operates through trial and error, slowly gaining an understanding of their practices. That said, individual experiences alone provide only a partial picture because they are limited to just a few aspects of the production process. For example, sending articles to journals and interacting with editors, responding to referees and correcting proofs, provide glimpses inside the 'black box' of journal publishing. However, without someone actually revealing how things work (for example, in a book like this), one only gets a real sense of how a medium truly operates when involved in other facets of production; for example, the full mechanics of journal production only become clear through working as an editor.

This book bypasses the need to learn about publication through personal experience, and attempts to lift the lid on the black boxes of dissemination to reveal how they operate. Drawing on our own experience and that of others, we discuss a range of forms of publication available to amateur and academic researchers, detailing their strengths and weaknesses, and outlining how to use them to let others know about your work. In addition, practical advice is supplied for those who want to take control of their own means of production (for example, self-publishing a report or book or newsletter) or who would like to take a more active role in the production process (such as starting a new journal). In doing so, the book provides a head start, detailing advice and knowledge that we would have valued when we started our careers as researchers.

2 A STRATEGIC APPROACH TO PUBLICATION

Given that there is a range of media through which research can potentially be published, and it is unlikely that you will have either the time or the inclination to explore all of them, there is a number of decisions that need to be made about the best outlets through which to showcase your work. These decisions, such as which journals to submit work to, or which conference to attend, will be shaped by two prime considerations. First, how and to whom do *you* want to communicate your work? Second (and increasingly, just as important), how and to whom do your *employers* or *funders* want the work disseminated? While there is often overlap, in that both you and those that sponsor your work will often want to target the same journals or conferences, it is often the case that there is some disagreement. For example, you might want to target a journal with a particular audience while your university administrators want you to submit to a journal with a high impact factor (as denoted by its citation index – see Chapter 6).

In the latter case, pressure arises from administrators because there continues to be perceived differences in the worth or value of academic work dependent on how it is disseminated. So the same work could, theoretically, be disseminated via a website, through a leading paper-based academic journal, or through the pages of an edited book, and be reviewed, consumed and valued in very different ways as a result. As noted in the Preface, this situation is exacerbated by the unrelenting neo-liberal restructuring of the education sector as certain modes of publication form the basis of calculative practices aimed at monitoring and regulating the endeavours of researchers.

Balancing individual preferences with institutional pressures requires a *strategic* approach to publication that utilizes particular tactics. A strategic approach means to have a consistent and planned method of dissemination that aims to fulfil defined goals. These goals might be to build a successful research career, to obtain employment, to gain tenure or pass probation, to achieve rapid promotion, to survive the academic system with as little effort as possible, to try to become famous, and so on. Tactics are the means for achieving these goals. These tactics might include submitting papers to the journals with the highest impact factor, attending the most prestigious conferences, organizing events, editing a newsletter, presenting at specialist conferences, sending press releases to the media, working with established researchers, and so on.

In our opinion, the key to achieving any lasting sense of personal academic satisfaction and freedom is to adopt a strategic approach to publication that works in *your* interests – in short, you need to develop your own strategy, a strategy that satisfies the 'rules of the game' but which maximizes *your* control over that game, and the time/resources available beyond it.

Of course, it is possible to be relatively successful employing a haphazard approach to publication, and there is no doubt that many researchers are quite haphazard in how they make their decisions on publication. For example, it can be quite easy to agree to submit an article to a particular journal or write a chapter for an edited book or attend a particular conference. But these choices might not be the best tactically in order to achieve one's goals. If these decisions involve taking on additional work then the time element in one's strategy will be altered radically. This approach, then, is far less likely to achieve one's goals than a strategic approach – it simply leaves too many things to chance and serendipity.

As suggested above, this is not to say that a strategic approach should be followed rigidly and in a heartless, calculated manner (there is little worse than joyless work). Rather, it is perhaps more sensible to employ a strategy that is flexible and which can react to situations as they arise. In other words, a productive strategy might be one that utilizes a minimum or adequate set of tactics to achieve a goal, but which leaves space and time to take on other interesting and rewarding commitments that also contribute towards this goal. This strategy ensures that defined targets are met, while not closing off new opportunities. An important tactic to keep such opportunities open, in an age when many institutions ask staff to set yearly work targets and then assess these targets at the end of the year, is not to over-estimate outputs. Over-estimating targets closes off new opportunities and places a researcher under pressure to deliver. In such a situation, a researcher either fails to deliver everything promised or reduces the standard of that delivered. It is much more sensible (and flattering) to be conservative or realistic and then to deliver or over-produce.

The strategy adopted and the tactics employed will often depend on what stage of your career you are at. As we explain below, if you are still a postgraduate and your goal is to gain a postdoctoral or teaching position then your strategy and associated tactics will almost certainly be very different from those if you are an already-established academic whose goal is to broaden your profile or rest on your laurels.

A postgraduate strategy

In today's competitive academic environment postgraduate students who want to continue their research career often need to adopt a strategy that separates them from the rest of their peers, and demonstrates that they can do more than merely survive the rigours of academic life (such as tenure-track and RAE – Research Assessment Exercise as operated in the UK – demands). While for many this is an unfortunate side effect of neo-liberal reforms to the higher education system, and the introduction of pernicious forms of academic capitalism, for the time being at least it remains a simple fact of life for would-be researchers. Gaining access to this environment necessitates employing tactics that stretch well beyond simply completing a competent PhD. Suitable tactics include: attending and presenting papers at regional, national and international conferences; getting involved in societies and organizations (for example, sitting on study group commit-tees); helping to organize meetings and conferences; editing newsletters or postgraduate/departmental journals; submitting papers to journals; and while not (directly) related to disseminating research, getting involved in teaching.

For postgraduates, the journals chosen for submissions do not neces-sarily need to be the ones considered the most important in a field. They might instead be departmental or society journals or 'lower ranking' jour-nals. The aim is to demonstrate potential and to build confidence. As we note below, the review process for many journals can be an unpleasant and upsetting experience. There is nothing worse than starting one's career with a series of rejection letters for articles that, while not quite good enough for the top journals, display scholarship that is worthy of publication. Similarly, when choosing conferences it is perhaps best to start with those that are more likely to provide a supportive environment for postgraduate students, such as postgraduate-only conferences, smaller regional and specialist conferences, and postgraduate sessions at major conferences.

Getting beyond contract research and teaching posts

For many researchers their route into a professional, tenured research career starts with a period of short-term research or teaching contracts. They have shown enough potential as a postgraduate to secure an initial step on the ladder. The next step is to secure a permanent position. This step is just as competitive as moving from postgraduate to postdoctoral level and again requires the adoption of tactics that distinguishes you from the rest of the crowd. Tactics that might be of benefit include publishing articles in specialist journals and in more generic, national and international journals (these do not necessarily have to be the top-rated journals, although a couple of articles in these would obviously do no harm!); attending and presenting at national and international conferences; being the main organizer of meetings and conferences; and taking an active role in disciplinary organizations. The aim is to demonstrate that you can achieve what is expected of a permanent member of staff: that you can publish in a variety of quality outlets, you are prepared to share your ideas at conferences and meetings, and that you care about and are prepared to be a steward for your discipline.

A tenure-track or probationary strategy

Tenure-track or probationary posts are those that lead to the relative job security of a tenured position. Tenure does not mean a permanent post that lasts until retirement; rather, tenure provides a right to a due process of evaluation prior to being fired. In other words, a college or university cannot terminate a post without presenting evidence that the professor is incompetent or unprofessional or that the finances that support a job are no longer sufficient (NEA, 2004). Until tenure is obtained, job security is very weak, with colleges and universities able to terminate a contract without reason or cause. A panel of senior professors and administrators, who evaluate the candidate's teaching, research and service, assesses tenure. The weight attached to these various assessment criteria varies depending on the institution, with research output and profile gaining more influence in top-ranked institutions. This assessment period can last between three and seven years depending on the type of educational institution and discipline. In the US and Canada, tenure is something that you pass, but this is not the same elsewhere. For example, in the UK probation (typically lasting three years) is something you fail. In other words, in the US and Canada you gain tenure, in the UK you are appointed to a tenured position from the start which you lose if you do not fulfil certain criteria. Whatever the system, there is no doubt probationary systems are complex, political and stressful. This is largely a function of the imbalance of power between the candidate and the panel of assessors, and the uncertainty of the outcome.

In relation to dissemination, a tenure committee generally expects the candidate to develop a portfolio of publications and presentations that, on the one hand, demonstrates the quality of the research being conducted (that is, by being accepted in top-rated journals) and, on the other, helps create a national and international profile. Typically the pressure will be for research articles in quality, international journals. In some disciplines, typically the Arts, Humanities and Social Sciences, it is expected that in the majority of cases, work will be single-authored or that the candidate is the first author. In some cases, panels might issue a list of suitable and non-suitable journals. They might even set specific targets of publishing papers in named journals or seek to block work that they deem unsuitable or see as less worthy or valuable than might be achieved.

For example, we know of tenure-track candidates who were strongly advised (in some cases, read forced) as follows: to give up writing a textbook (because it was perceived to lack academic, as opposed to pedagogic, value); to give up writing a monograph and convert the chapters into journal articles (because the supposed combined value of the articles would be more than the book); to change which journals they intended to submit their articles to (because the committee felt the journals chosen by the candidate did not have a high enough impact factor); and to attend certain conferences as opposed to others (because the candidate would be mixing with a 'better class' or more international mix of attendees). As a consequence, tenure/probation can be quite a constraining time, with patterns of work to some degree directed by those that assess tenure rather than being self-directed. That said, there is often quite a bit of latitude to make decisions on the focus of research, academic activities and the means of publication. If this is the case, we would advise that these decisions should be made strategically and in line with the recommendations of the tenure panel.

It can be difficult to follow committee advice, especially when it is very disciplining and constraining. The instinct is often to rebel and follow one's own path. This might not prove to be a problem if that path produces results and benefits that the tenure committee is going to appreciate (such as articles in top journals). The danger is, however, that it will alienate the committee and turn them against you. Given the imbalance of power, this is likely to be a dangerous and potentially costly approach. Perhaps the best advice, therefore, is to 'play the game' (for the time being at least), doing as much as needed by the committee, while using any spare time or energies to pursue your own agendas and tactics.

 ## After-tenure strategies

While securing tenure or probation seems to provide the academic freedom to pursue whatever publication strategy desired, it remains the case that you are still accountable to your employer (most likely a university). This is particularly the case if you wish to progress your career, as research outputs play an important role in judging applications for promotion, and salary and merit increases. In this respect, university administrators will expect you to continue to develop and expand your international, research profile. It is true, however, that there is much more scope to explore different forms of publication, such as writing and editing books or writing policy-orientated reports, without necessarily feeling the same pressures and penalties that might have existed at earlier stages in your career. Which strategy is employed is really dependent on goals, which at this stage of a career are almost all self-selected and directed.

That said, institutional pressures to successfully and strategically publish research in particular ways regardless of career stage are growing. Further pressures are created in other ways. For example, it might be that pressures arise from collaborative working relationships where partners are at different stages of their career (with one partner pressuring another to deliver). There is also the pressure to keep one's curriculum vitae full of new additions to enable career progression from one employer to another. Moreover, the extent to which we, as academics, pressurize, exploit and discipline ourselves, and each other, also seems to be increasing, as universities become more competitive places to work (see Fuller and Kitchin, 2004). Perhaps this stage is seemingly more comfortable to some because by this point pressure, exploitation and disciplining have become the norm – we have learned to conform and play the game.

A strategy to deal with RAE or other forms of research accountancy

The Research Assessment Exercise (RAE) in the UK, and other forms of pernicious research accountancy in operation in other countries, are having profound effects on the strategies and tactics of publishing required of researchers. These exercises seek to measure the 'quality', 'usefulness', 'impact' and 'value-for-money' of research through the evaluation of research outputs. Typically they examine a sample or all of a researcher's work, judging it through a reading by 'experts', by how and where it was published, or by how many times it has been cited – or a combination of these. Each exercise is accompanied by a rationale and its mode of measurement is pre-circulated so that researchers generally know what to expect.

In recent years, the RAE in the UK has required research staff to submit four pieces of what they consider to be their 'best' published work from the previous four or five years. It is expected that these pieces of work will consist of refereed articles in international journals that have a high citation index or research monographs published and distributed by international publishing houses. This is not to say that other forms of publication will not be considered, rather that these forms are generally expected as they are perceived to denote 'quality' and are much more likely to have a wider, global impact. Almost inevitably this means writing in English, because English-language publishing houses dominate international publishing and English has become *the* language of global intellectual discourse and science. What these measures mean is that consultant reports, pamphlets, papers in regional, national, non-English or lower-ranked journals, online articles, magazine and newspaper articles, conference papers published in proceedings, websites, and textbooks for both school and university level, take on less 'worth' in such evaluative systems. Moreover, it is generally only written works that are seen to 'count', with other forms of publication such as conference presentations and media coverage being seen as relatively 'valueless'. This, however, varies between countries and assessment scheme.

Such exercises can place researchers under enormous institutional and peer pressure to deliver certain forms of prescribed research output, as it is not simply the individual that is rewarded or penalized, but the whole department (whose budget is dependent on collective performance). In turn these exercises can lead to the (self-)disciplining of academics through the creation of institutional systems that reward the 'right' kinds of publication (through rapid promotion, access to research monies, stable employment) and punish those that fail to do so (through discontinuation of employment, stalled career paths, higher teaching and/or administrative loads, and so on). In this kind of environment researchers need to adopt a strategy that minimizes stresses and outcomes that hinder their research and maximizes benefits and the freedom to pursue their academic and career goals. The simplest way to achieve this balance is to fulfil the minimum criteria of assessment, providing the freedom to then pursue publication strategies designed to fulfil other goals. These other strategies, to a greater or lesser degree, will still potentially contribute to assessment criteria, perhaps replacing other work due to be assessed. Of course this strategy to cope with an assessment exercise is reliant on being able to fulfil the minimum criteria of assessment. If, as time passes, this looks increasingly unlikely, then another strategy is needed.

A strategy to deal with setbacks and failures

As Chapter 1 detailed, successful publication requires certain knowledges and skills; it is certainly not assured. A project might be a great success and produce useful empirical material and theoretic ideas, but if you do not know what the conduit of publication expects (and thereby transgress rules concerning submission and production) or your work fails to meet specific criteria and standards (such as focus, format, style, length, standard of argument and evidence, standard of language, grammar and punctuation, and so on), then it can be difficult to get work accepted by editors and publishers and distributed.

If you are having difficulty getting material accepted for publication, the first thing that needs to be done is a review of your tactics and experiences. Submitted work is very rarely rejected by publishers, editors, conference organizers and so on without reason. It is true that some work can be rejected for the wrong reasons, but again this is relatively rare. More usually the problem lies in a mismatch between the submitted work and the need to follow the 'rules of the game'. For example, the most common reasons articles submitted to journals are rejected are: the topic was not appropriate to the journal foci; the argumentation and evidence presented was weak or unconvincing; the narrative of the article was poor in comparison to what was expected; or the article failed to make connections to other relevant literature and therefore lacked context. Similar and other reasons relate to book proposals, conferences and so on, and are discussed in each relevant chapter. Comments from editors and referees, while often painful to read, do give valuable advice that will explain where they think you are going wrong in relation to the 'rules'. You might not agree with all of the comments, but it is almost certain that some of them will have merit when viewed against the expected rubric. Work through these comments alongside your submitted work and reflect on how the piece might have been improved to meet their criticism. It might also be useful to ask friends and colleagues to take a look at the work and referees' comments and give you their reflections. The aim is to try to learn from the experience.

The second thing that needs to happen is for you to use the findings from your review to change your future tactics of publication. If the reason your work is being rejected is that it does not follow the brief of submission, then find the relevant guidelines and follow them in future. If the standard of writing is affecting whether a piece of work is accepted, then work hard to improve the deficiencies. If need be, read books on how to improve your writing style (see Chapter 4) or attend a writing course . If your book proposal is being rejected for being too parochial then think about how the text might be broadened to have wider appeal. If your articles are being rejected by the top journals in the field, which often have high rejection rates and only accept the work of the highest quality, then perhaps think about submitting to lower-rated journals, thus building up your experience and confidence. In other words, use the feedback you receive and your experiences to learn and adapt.

The following chapters provide specific advice in relation to the different forms of dissemination available to meet whatever needs you have.

REFERENCES

Fuller, D. and Kitchin, R. (2004) 'Radical theory/critical praxis', in D. Fuller and R. Kitchin (eds), *Radical Theory, Critical Praxis: Making a Difference Beyond the Academy?* Praxis E-Press. http://www.praxis-epress.org/rtcp/contents.html, pp. 1–20.

NEA (2004) *The Truth About Tenure in Higher Education.* http://www.nea.org/he/truth.html. Last accessed 4 August 2004.

3 WORKING WITH OTHERS

Research is often a collaborative venture undertaken by two or more colleagues. What this means is that project work and publication is reliant on teamwork. This teamwork can take different forms, such as members undertaking set tasks or working together on tasks. Collaboration can be enormously rewarding intellectually, socially and with respect to one's career. And just as there are benefits, there are also issues to be aware of. There is little point pretending that academia is not a pressured and competitive environment, or that personalities and ambitions do not play a role in academic endeavour. As a consequence, collaborations are *always* under threat from both internal and external tensions. People come to projects at different points in their careers, and are often in the process of employing strategies designed to achieve divergent goals. Collaborative partners can have different priorities, whether that be other projects, other academic jobs such as administration, or home life. In addition, the circumstances of partners may change over the course of a project, for example due to a new more exciting project coming on stream, changing jobs, or having children.

In nearly every collaborative venture, contributions vary in terms of time and effort, and the work across members is often of variable quality. What this means is that some contributors may feel that they are contributing more or are 'carrying' other members, particularly if workloads deviate substantially from that agreed. This can breed resentment and mistrust. The project can also get very politicized because members have vested interests in relation to developing their profile, promotion and so on.

With regard to publication, there can be differences of opinion in terms of how and through what media the work should be disseminated. In addition, there are a number of issues you should be aware of concerning who should be listed as authors on a piece of work and the ordering of names (see Chapter 5). While these issues are really administrative, and concern energies, priorities and efforts, there are other issues that are perhaps more difficult to resolve. These include a clash of personalities and also fundamental differences with respect to theoretic ideas, interpretation of empirical materials and working styles (which in relation to dissemination might be writing style).

Remember, just because a collaboration is between friends does not guarantee its success; being friends and being able to work together are quite different things. We would be the first to admit that we have had to work hard at nurturing the collaboration that produced this book despite being good friends and having worked together for several years previously. Booth et al. (2003) suggest three tactics for working together successfully:

- *Talk a lot*: adopt a pattern of regular correspondence, swapping ideas and points of view.
- *Agree to disagree*: do not expect to agree on every issue, keep disagreements in perspective, and be prepared to compromise.
- *Organize and plan*: create roles for each person and make sure there is an agreed plan of action, with one person designated as the coordinator/moderator.

They also suggest three strategies to progress group work:

- *Divide and delegate*: tasks are parcelled out to individual group members who work on them individually or in smaller groups until complete.
- *Work side by side*: tasks are tackled collectively, with members working closely with each other.
- *Take turns*: a task is passed from each member of the group, with each adding something to it.

Most groups use a combination of these strategies at different stages of a project.

For collaborative ventures to be a success they need to be planned carefully and worked at, and they should not be entered into lightly. Remember each collaboration will probably last several years (the initial research and then the phase of publication). Each partner needs to know what the others bring to the venture. Each should be clear on their role and what is expected of them in terms of tasks, time and effort, and that of the others. In short, the secret of a strong collaborative venture is a shared mindset, good, open communication, transparent working relationships and partners fulfilling their obligations. This is particularly the case when partners are working at a distance and do not regularly see each other, or if the collaboration consists of teams located at different sites.

If, in your opinion, a collaborative venture is progressing badly then the best course of action in the first instance is discussion and negotiation. While suffering in silence might be an option politically (say because of a power imbalance, with one of the partners holding control of resourcing or staffing), it is certainly not a long-term solution. In this case, it might be prudent to discuss the matter privately (rather than with the whole group) to see whether conditions and arrangements can be altered to your satisfaction. Otherwise, organize a group meeting to discuss what you perceive to be the problems and what the solutions might be. In either case, be prepared to make some kind of compromise and to recognize the views or positions of others.

If discussion fails to resolve critical issues, then the next stage is some kind of arbitration. Nobody wants to walk away from work that they have invested time and energy into. Moreover, if the research is funded the funding agency will want to see the project completed and the findings published. Non-completion or inadequate publication might result in sanctions against team members or institutions. By bringing in an 'independent' person or panel a fresh and critical perspective can be brought to bear on any problems. They can mediate the discussion and suggest potential solutions. This might consist of clarifying any misunderstandings or renegotiating workloads or jobs or coming to an agreement as to how the project can be separated into new ventures. In relation to publication, the latter might mean deciding how collaborative writing can be untangled into new writing projects.

If arbitration does not work then the final resort is terminating the collaborative venture. Termination can be quite amicable, with parties separating with agreed understandings of how they might progress the work individually. It can also be extremely messy and can have legal consequences, especially if the work involved contracts. Our advice is to avoid legal proceedings unless there is no other option. They can be costly both financially and in terms of a career, and extremely stressful.

REFERENCES

Booth, W.C., Colomb, G.G. and Williams, J.M. (2003) *The Craft of Research*, 2nd edn. Chicago: University of Chicago Press.

4   GENERAL WRITING ADVICE

Writing is principally about the effective communication of ideas and observations. Good communicative writing is a skill. It is rare for somebody to be a 'naturally' skilled writer and most authors learn their craft through experience and the help of others (for example, those who read, review and correct their scripts). In this chapter we provide some general, overarching guidelines and advice that will help to improve the effectiveness of your writing. Specific advice about writing for different media is provided in subsequent chapters.

● Appropriate writing

The first principle of good writing is to write for, on the one hand, the intended audience and, on the other, the medium of dissemination. Usually these are highly interconnected, in that media are targeted at specific audiences. Audiences differ in their knowledge of a topic, their intellectual ability and their interest. Writing for a specialist expert audience who are likely to read an academic journal is very different from writing a pedagogic text used for teaching, which is different again from writing for a specialist magazine aimed at a lay readership or a newspaper article aimed at a very broad, non-specialist audience. In each case, not only does the audience vary, but also the medium of communication, with the language, terms used and writing style required being distinct.

Effective communication, then, requires writing at a level and in a style appropriate to convey your ideas and findings to a particular audience. It also entails writing in a way that is appropriate to a particular medium and coincides with what the production team expect. What this means in practice is that an author needs to develop a quite sophisticated sense of who the target audience is and what is an appropriate level and style of communication. At the same time, an author needs to know how a medium works and how to exploit that medium effectively. Time invested developing such knowledge is time well spent. It will help produce well-written texts that will be well received by editors and reviewers and it will increase the chance that texts will be accepted for publication.

 ## Standard

The second principle for achieving well-received writing is to write to a professional standard. This does not mean to write to a level, using complex terms and phrasing, where only a few 'experts' will understand arguments and findings. It means that the text *reads* well; that it is well presented, clearly structured, has a strong narrative flow, is grammatically correct and has an unambiguous message. It is true that standards of English and argument do often vary across media, but as a writer you should seek to maintain a basic high standard of writing, keeping in mind audience and medium. There are a number of ways to ensure a high standard of writing.

Grammar and punctuation

Every type of written communication has rules concerning its form and format. These rules relate to grammar and punctuation. The publishing industry expects authors to be familiar with these rules and to obey them, as they require texts that are grammatically correct, with the proper syntax. Publishers employ copy-editing staff who check and correct grammar and punctuation, but given the costs involved they will not re-draft text for an author. The onus, then, is on the author to submit texts that meet the standards required.

Grammar is a set of rules and guidelines concerned with the use of language. It refers to basic parts of sentence construction, such as nouns, pronouns, adjectives, verbs, adverbs, prepositions, conjunctions and interjections, and to tense and phrasing. A text with weak grammar can be very difficult to interpret because the sentences are largely nonsensical.

Punctuation is the syntax used in sentence construction. Basic punctuation devices include commas, full stops, ellipses, semi-colons, colons, apostrophes, brackets and question and exclamation marks. Punctuation provides the reader with a structure that aids interpretation. Poor punctuation can make a sentence difficult to comprehend or even change its meaning.

Grammar and punctuation combined provide the rules for creating sentences. Sentences are the building blocks of a text; if an author's sentences are confusing or nonsensical, then the overall text will be too. For novice writers, basic errors in grammar and punctuation are often the most common problem. Perhaps the most frequent mistake for seasoned authors is to place too many sub-clauses within one sentence. There is nothing wrong in this in itself, but it tends to make the sentence very long, with clauses and sense becoming confused. In addition, a seasoned writer can become complacent, so that a disparity emerges between intention and execution; what one thinks one has said is not what one has actually written (Palmer, 2002). In other words, even experienced writers need to check their writing carefully for punctuation and grammatical errors. At the very least you should become adept at operating whatever spelling and grammar checking system you have available on your computer (though never become overly reliant on these as they are not foolproof!).

Narrative and structure

The key to ensuring good 'readability' is a well-structured text with a strong narrative. Any text, whether factually based or fiction, should read like a story; there should be a beginning, a middle and an end, with a strong, coherent plot-line running throughout linking all the intervening sentences and sections. A piece of writing that fails to have a strong narrative, and which lacks a logical structure to lead the reader through the text, will be difficult and frustrating to read.

Narrative flow and structure need to work at all levels of the text; it applies as much to the ordering and linking of sentences as it does to paragraphs, sections and chapters. A common mistake among novice writers is a failure to link pieces of text. Sometimes sentences or paragraphs seem to be randomly arranged. As a result, despite the fact that the argument and evidence being presented might be important, the narrative is halting and confused. In these cases, poor structure and narrative detract from the worth of the work being reported, and will almost certainly prevent it being published until major revisions are undertaken.

A cohesive, coherent text is one where each sentence links to the next, each paragraph to the one previous, and so on. Flow is created by there being a slight overlap in content and message; they reinforce each other. Williams (2003) suggests that there are four components to a coherent text:

- Readers can see the main point of your text.
- They understand the relevance of its parts to that point.
- They recognize the principle behind the order of those parts.
- They are encouraged by your text to read purposefully and attentively.

Let us draw these points out a little more. The reader must be able to clearly identify the main point you are trying to make. In turn, each paragraph and section must have a point of its own that contributes to the overall point. The text must be ordered so that points build on each other in sequence and points must be stated in a way that motivates a reader to read on. Booth et al. (2003) detail three motivators that will sell an essay to a reader, the third of which is most common in academic research. The author conveys to the reader:

- I've found something really interesting
- I've found a solution to a practical problem that's important to you, and/or
- I've found an answer to a question that's important to you.

In terms of the ordering, Williams (2003: 211–12) details three ways in which a text can be arranged: coordinate, chronological and logical.

- *Coordinate*: two or more sections are coordinate with one another when they are like pillars supporting a roof. 'There are three reasons why . . .', and each section discusses a reason for supporting a point. These sections are themselves ordered by importance, complexity, and so on.
- *Chronological*: parts are ordered from earlier to later.
- *Logical*: parts are ordered by example and generalization (or vice versa), premise and conclusion, or assertion and contradiction.

The end of one part and the beginning of a next should be signalled clearly using signalling words (such as, first, second, . . . or therefore, in contrast, etc.) or (sub)headings.

The two most effective methods to ensure both flow and structure are careful thought and planning in advance of drafting a manuscript, and a willingness to revise and edit the draft repeatedly until a satisfactory text is produced. Two good tactics to test the style and structure of an initial draft are to read the text aloud and to get friends/colleagues/supervisors to read and comment on the paper. Both tactics will quickly identify any major problems.

○ Clarity and style

Working hard at both grammar and punctuation, and narrative and structure, tends to create a high degree of clarity in a text: ideas, argument and evidence can be clearly understood by the reader. It does not, however, ensure it. This is because a script always appears clearer to the writer than the reader. The writer reads into the text the meaning intended when written, an advantage that the reader lacks and which can only be inferred from the text presented. If that meaning is not explicitly spelled out, then the reader can misinterpret text (which is why having friends or colleagues read a draft of the text is so useful; they can point out the problems). An author then must work hard to minimize ambiguity by creating a text that has clarity.

There is no doubt that some ideas and arguments are complex and difficult to explain. Skilled writers can, however, communicate this complexity clearly and without creating unnecessary confusion. Writing a complex argument in a complex manner is relatively easy, drafting it in a way that minimizes ambiguity takes time and effort. Unfortunately, many researchers' texts are verbose, dense and frustrating to read. They perhaps confuse such writing with demonstrating sophisticated thinking. Or perhaps they think that texts that need to be worked at by the reader to be understood are more valued. It is our opinion that those who create such deflective arguments are either too lazy or too busy to revise their writing, or think that elaborate phrasing will impress. When faced with a text that needs to be read repeatedly in order for it to be understood, most readers actually give up rather than persevere.

Clarity should never be confused with simplicity; just because the argument within an essay is clear and well explained, does not mean that it is simple. It means the writer has done an exceptional job to explain a complex argument with clarity. You should aim to be this kind of writer; one that people will enjoy reading.

Stylistically, journal and commissioning editors are looking for texts that are accessible to the reader, with conceptual ideas and empirical data clearly described and explained. They will expect formal English to be used; that is, no slang, no colloquialisms and no contractions (I'm, don't, isn't, etc.). They will be particularly happy to receive texts that are engaging to read and draw the reader in, rather than something that is competent, but dry and dull.

Academic conventions about writing in the third person are changing and many editors and publishers will now accept pieces written in the first person. In all instances, editors and publishers will expect authors to *follow the formatting guidelines as set out in the notes for contributors/authors* (printed in each issue of a journal or supplied by a book publisher – and in both cases increasingly available online). These provide specific details concerning the length, format and content of prospective manuscripts.

◯ Writing to length

In order to balance costs and the content of periodicals, publishers and editors set word lengths on submissions. While some are stricter than others, they expect these limits to be adhered to and they hold the right to reject a submission that fails to meet length criteria. It is therefore good practice to write a text so it conforms to length requirements.

Many authors find trying to meet length requirements restrictive and frustrating. It is usually the case that they feel they have a lot of important things to say and require more space than is available. Certainly one of the most common requests of editors is for authors to reduce the word count. Some authors can become quite precious about their writing if this request occurs. They will often argue that they cannot possibly explain fully their work or do the project justice in a shorter piece. This is simply not the case. It is possible to say a lot in few words and a useful exercise to illustrate this is to write the text as if for several different media. So, for example, write a full article for an academic journal as desired; write the same piece for an academic periodical that only accepts short articles; draft a submission of the same work for a specialist lay magazine, and then for a newspaper. In each case, the central argument and points should remain the same, but the space in which to convey them is drastically reduced. A skilled writer will manage to communicate the core argument and points in each case. In other words, it is a poor, undisciplined writer who cannot write for the space available.

There are several strategies that can be used to reduce the length of a text. They all require you to try to determine what material is and is not essential to your argument. Take the following steps:

- Remove any unnecessary text (for example, qualifying or repetitive words).
- Summarize passages of text into one or two sentences.

- Delete references and quotations that are not essential to the discussion.
- Replace lengthy descriptions by tables and charts where possible.
- Remove whole sections, or perhaps even chapters, where these are not central to the argument.

If in doubt, then ask the following questions: 'Is this sentence/paragraph/section important to the development of my argument?' and 'What would be lost if I left it out?' If you are still having trouble reducing the length, then you are probably trying to say too much in one piece and you should consider dividing the text to create two or more new essays.

⃝ Tables, figures, plates, maps

Tables, figures, plates and maps can be extremely useful for conveying information or illustrating a point. However, they should only be used *when relevant* and must be *referred to* in the text.

Place markers for tables, figures, plates and maps should be included at appropriate points in the text (for example, 'Figure 1 about here') but the items themselves should be included on separate sheets at the end of the manuscript.

You should consult specific journals' notes for contributors about exact formatting, but, following Kitchin and Tate (1998), do the following for all tables, figures, plates and maps:

- Provide an appropriate title.
- Display it at an appropriate size so that visual interpretation is easy and the text is readable.
- Give an acknowledgement immediately underneath if it is taken from another source.
- Supply an explanatory legend.

For tables

- Label every column and row with appropriate titles (including data units).
- Column headings should refer to independent variables and row headings to dependent variables.
- If the data are numeric then use appropriate decimal places and be

consistent. For missing data insert n.a., an abbreviation of 'not available'.

- Format the table so that stronger lines demarcate specific rows and columns, and ensure columns are appropriately spaced and that interpretation is easy.

For figures

- Make sure the message the figure is trying to convey is clear and unambiguous.
- Make sure the figure is uncluttered and is as simple as possible.

For plates

- Ensure that the plate is of high quality in terms of image resolution and contrast.
- Reproduce it at a size appropriate to the level of detail required by the reader.

For graphs

- Label both axes with appropriate titles and provide units of measurement for each axis.
- The independent variable should be plotted on the horizontal axis and the dependent variable on the vertical axis.
- Use appropriate scales on each axis.
- Make sure different data sets are clearly distinguishable and are identified by a key.

For maps

- Make sure the map is uncluttered and contains the necessary information at an appropriate scale.
- Include a scale bar and north arrow.

For advice on map-making see Robinson et al. (1995).

 # Language

Most English language publishers will only accept submissions that are written in formal English. There are a few exceptions that might allow a text to be submitted and reviewed in a different language. If accepted for publication, however, they most probably will require the submission to be translated into English (usually at the expense of the author).

Title

Choosing a title is an important, but often overlooked, concern. Potential readers often judge whether to read an article, book, report and so on on the basis of its title. The main title should include words that indicate the key theme of the published work. The subtitle, if used, should indicate the specific focus examined or argument advanced. There are different styles of titles that convey different messages. They range from the authoritative through to the witty.

Epigraph

An epigraph is a quotation that is placed at the start of a paper, chapter or section that makes a point or sets the scene for what follows. It should be a thought-provoking foil for what follows. An epigraph should be chosen with care and only used if it adds to the argument made. Its message should be self-explanatory but if any elaboration is needed it should follow in the text.

Statistical formulae

Beyond simple mathematical operations such as addition, subtraction etc., all statistical formulae used should be included. These should use the full form and should be fully defined. Although strictly speaking new terms will only need to be defined on their first appearance in the text, subsequent inclusions may increase the clarity of a complicated equation.

Quoting

If you are using another author's exact words, even if it is just a short phrase, then the quoted text needs to be enclosed with quote marks, the author cited along with the page number from which the quote is taken, and the full reference detailed according to the referencing style (see below).

Failing to declare that the piece of text is taken from another source is a form of plagiarism (see Chapter 5). If the quote is short, it is generally retained in the main text. For example:

> For Judith Butler, gender and what it means to be a woman or man is produced and sustained through acts, gestures, mannerisms, clothing and so on; that is, gender is performed; it is 'the repeated stylization of the body' (Butler, 1990: 43).

However, if the quote is longer (normally 40 words or more) or has particular relevance, it may be separated from the main text and indented in smaller type to distinguish it from your writing. If the quote is indented, quote marks are not always required. For example:

As Judith Butler (1990: 43–4) argues:

> Gender is the repeated stylization of the body, a set of repeated acts within a highly rigid regulatory frame that congeal over time to produce the appearance of substance, of a natural sort of being.

If the text is taken from a source such as the Internet, it is likely to have no page numbers. In this case, replace the page number with the phrase 'no pagination'. If you want to emphasize a particular part of the quote, use italics and acknowledge that the emphasis is yours not the original author's. For example:

> Gender is the *repeated stylization* of the body, a set of repeated acts within a highly rigid regulatory frame that congeal over time to produce the appearance of substance, of a natural sort of being. (Butler, 1990: 43–4, our emphasis)

If you want to miss out a bit of the quote, then use an ellipsis – '. . .' – to denote the words cut. For example:

> For Judith Butler, '[g]ender is the repeated stylization of the body . . . repeated acts . . . that congeal over time to produce the appearance of substance' (Butler, 1990: 43–4).

Note the use of square brackets here to denote that the case of the letter 'g' has been changed.

As a general rule you should use quotes from other texts sparingly, employing them:

- When you are examining in detail another person's work which is open to interpretation.
- When the quoted material provides a specific example useful for the argument you are making and/or
- When the quoted material provides eloquent phrasing that emphasizes your point.

In all other cases, it is expected that reference to another author's work will be paraphrased, and cited accordingly, so that text is framed within your view and maintains an even style.

Citing

All material that has been derived from other sources must be referenced within the text and fully recorded in a reference list or as footnotes or endnotes. Failure to cite material is plagiarism (see Chapter 5). There are various different ways to acknowledge the ideas of others within the text. These are often referred to as 'styles of documentation' (see the *Chicago Manual of Style* (1993) for comprehensive source of different styles). The rules and form of documentation vary between journals and publishers; however, three general forms are common:

- Endnotes – number citations in the text referring to notes at the end of the text, e.g.
  Gender is something one does, rather than something one is.[1]
- Footnotes – number citations in the text referring to notes at the bottom of each page (sometimes complemented with full lists of references at the end of the text) e.g.
  Gender is something one does, rather than something one is.[1]
- Author–date citations – author's name, publication date and page numbers in the text (where quoting), with the full reference at the end of the text, e.g.
  Gender is something one does, rather than something one is (Butler, 1990).

Referencing

Referencing consists of providing full and accurate details on the sources of information referred to in the text. The information is supplied in footnotes, endnotes or as a reference list. Many different styles of documentation are used to provide references in published material and the 'notes for contributors/authors' provided by a publisher should be consulted to determine the exact format required in each specific case. These should be followed exactly and consistently using all the correct punctuation (full stops, commas, colons, abbreviations, etc.) and font style (e.g., italics or bold). The following examples are how references to different media should be formatted for the journal *Social and Cultural Geography* (whose notes for contributors are supplied by the publisher at http://www.tandf.co.uk/journals/authors/rscgauth.asp). If you compare these with the references in other books you can see how publishers' house styles can vary with regard to punctuation, but the elements required are the same.

Book
Jackson, P. (1989) *Maps of Meaning*. London: Routledge.

Journal article
Anderson, K. (1987) The idea of Chinatown: the power of place and institutional practice in the making of a racial category, *Annals of the Association of American Geographers* 77: 127–49.

Chapter in an edited book
Parr, H. and Philo, C. (1995) Mapping mad identities, in Pile, S. and Thrift, N. (eds), *Mapping the Subject: Geographies of Cultural Transformation*. London: Routledge, pp. 199–225.

Dissertation
Kneale, J. (1996) *Lost in Space?: Readers' Constructions of Science Fiction Worlds*, PhD dissertation, Department of Geography, University College London.

Newspaper article
O'Morain, P. (1998) Differences between North, South lie in access to services for disabled, *The Irish Times*, 5 October.

Material published on the Internet
U.S.–Canada Power System Outage Task Force. (2004) Final report on the August 14th blackout in the United States and Canada. https://reports.energy.gov/ Last accessed 29th June 2004.

Acknowledgements

It is very rare for a text to be written in a social and intellectual vacuum and it is customary to acknowledge the formative inputs of others to the final, published piece of work. This might include friends or colleagues who provided advice, feedback and support on earlier drafts of the piece, independent referees or reviewers who made constructive criticism on previously submitted versions, and the (journal or book) editor who guided the manuscript through submission and production. If the material being published was supported financially by a bursary or grant it is usually mandatory to acknowledge such support by detailing the name of the funding agency, the title of the project and, if applicable, the award number.

 # General writing mistakes

Beyond writing for a specific audience and medium, and general issues that relate to the standard of writing (narrative and structure, grammar and punctuation, etc.), there is a number of common mistakes that lead to a poor text.

Padding

Padding consists of including text that adds little or nothing to the central arguments being made. It tends to detract from or obscure the main points and it also slows down or diverts the narrative flow. As a consequence it makes the text less enjoyable to read. What Palmer (2002: 76) refers to as 'deliberate fleshiness' is often a particular problem in academic writing. This involves employing a style to impress, intimidate or conceal, usually through the use of verbose and sophisticated vocabulary. Palmer (2002: 76) suggests three main forms: 'excessive abstraction; indifference to clarity and the reader's comfort; self-indulgent verbosity'. All three should be avoided. Rather than pad out a text for the sake of making minor points or to make the work longer or create false impressiveness, it is much better to keep the narrative clear, tight and focused. A piece that is short, snappy and to the point will be much better received than one that is long, dull and verbose, with the message hidden.

◯ Repetition

A quite common mistake in texts is repetition, literally the repeating of sentences, phrases or points. It is usually the product of poor structure or the labouring of a point. The solution is strong editing and/or restructuring that will consolidate related text into one part of the piece.

◯ Making too many points

A relatively common mistake, especially among inexperienced authors, is to try to cram too much into a text. This is particularly the case for journal articles where quite strict word limits often apply. Effective texts are those that communicate one or two points well. Cramming lots of points into one text detracts from the central arguments being made and can make a text bitty and confusing. The solution is strong editing. Those points removed are not wasted; they form a useful start to another piece of writing.

◯ Making too few points

The converse problem is a text that says too little. In the age of 'publish or perish' it is often tempting to try to milk a project for every potential paper (see Chapter 5). What can happen in this situation is that rather than producing, say, four very good substantial papers, an author can be seduced into placing the same material into eight, slight papers. As a result none of the papers has any substantive intellectual weight and the impact of the work can be diluted. If the main point being developed in each paper becomes quite minor through such stretching of material, then it will also be difficult to get a paper accepted for publication.

● Finally

Do not put the product of your labours in the post as soon as it is finished. If at all possible, put it to one side for at least two weeks, then give it another look. This 'cooling off' period means you return to your work afresh, ready to assess the coherence of your arguments, spot errors and tidy up inconsistencies. One last read-through checking for errors from start to finish should follow this.

REFERENCES

Booth, W.C., Colomb, G.G. and Williams, J.M. (2003) *The Craft of Research*, 2nd edn. Chicago: University of Chicago Press.

Butler, J. (1990) *Gender Trouble*. London: Routledge.

Chicago Manual of Style (1993) 14th Edition. Chicago: University of Chicago Press.

Kitchin, R. and Tate, N. (1998) *Conducting Research in Human Geography: Theory, Methodology and Practice*. Harlow: Prentice Hall.

Palmer, R. (2002) *Write in Style: A Guide to Good English*, 2nd edn. London: Routledge.

Robinson, A.H., Morrison, J.L., Muehrcke, P.C., Kimerling, A.J. and Guptil, S.C. (1995) *Elements of Cartography*, 5th edn. New York: John Wiley.

Williams, J.M. (2003) *Style: Ten Lessons in Clarity and Grace*, 7th edn. New York: Longman.

5 MALPRACTICES AND INTELLECTUAL PROPERTY

In addition to general advice concerning the skills of writing there is a number of other related issues that every writer needs to be aware of. These issues are generally legal or political in nature and cannot be ignored as they have penalties (of different kinds) attached. It is better to be forewarned than to find out about these problems at a later date, once it is too late.

Plagiarism and other malpractices

The re-use and reworking of other people's empirical and theoretical research is a central aspect of academic endeavour. New work builds on old, incrementally pushing forward, challenging and constructing new theories and ways of doing research. No research occurs in a vacuum and is entirely unique. Instead, research is built, sometimes obliquely, other times more obviously, on the various ideas and work of those who have informed the education of the researcher. Indeed, the whole point of publishing academic work is to make it public to allow others to examine and evaluate the work and to see how it might inform their own thinking.

Plagiarism, however, consists of a number of related practices that interfere with the public record and which can result in, at the best, acute embarrassment and, at worst and more likely, disciplining by the institution that employs you and prosecution for the theft of intellectual property. Indeed, it is fair to say that the various forms of plagiarism are considered among the worst offences an academic can commit.

In terms of academic publishing, the main forms of plagiarism are copying, parallelism, passing and duplication.

○ Copying

Copying is effectively the theft of somebody else's ideas, data or analysis. It usually consists of verbatim copying of text from another source and claiming it as one's own. As noted above, it is expected that a published work will refer to the work of others, but it is also expected that the author will acknowledge that previous work. If you wish to reproduce a piece of text verbatim, then it has to appear in your text as a quote (see Chapter 4).

○ Parallelism

Parallelism is the paraphrasing of somebody else's work without acknowledging the source of the ideas, in effect claiming it as one's own. In other words, your text is written in your own words, but somebody else initially formulated what is being said. Here, the intellectual contribution of the work that you are drawing on to make your point needs to be acknowledged in your text (see Chapter 4). Clearly, however, very few ideas are absolutely 'new', and so some common sense also needs to be applied to avoid over-referencing:

○ Passing

Passing is another form of intellectual theft, wherein although the author might have undertaken some of the analysis and written up the work – which is not copied from another source – the content of the piece is fully or in-part based on the research of others, such as colleagues or research assistants. In other words, the author is trying to pass off the intellectual property of others as solely their own. As a general rule, if a piece of work is based on the intellectual work of others, or was written collaboratively, then the names of *all* parties should be included in the list of authors.

In some cases passing might be deemed acceptable depending on how much work different people contributed to the written piece and if all parties have agreed to the arrangement. For example, it is not uncommon for authors to publish work in which the data generation and analysis was undertaken by a research assistant, but where the assistant is not credited on the paper. This is usually in cases where the author was responsible for all the intellectual aspects of the project, determining how the data were to be generated and analysed, and providing the interpretation of findings. Here, the assistant has invested little intellectually to the project as it has been conceived in total by the author (although the assistant's contribution will be noted in an acknowledgements section). If, however, the assistant has been instrumental to the intellectual endeavour, then one would expect that person to be listed as an author.

Similarly, it is generally accepted that somebody who reads through a script and corrects spelling mistakes and grammar, and/or who makes some suggestions with regards to restructuring or reworking an idea, will not be listed as a contributing author (although their contribution will be noted in an acknowledgements section). However, if this person actually does some re-writing or adds substantive new material, then they are actively co-writing the script and they should become a named author. The order of names in both cases usually reflects the level of contribution of each author. However, where a PhD supervisor publishes the work of a student as his or her own, without crediting the student, the student will have contributed considerably to the intellectual content of the project and the supervisor is guilty of passing, of stealing, the student's ideas.

Our suggestion is to make sure that everyone involved in the project is happy with the list of named authors *before* you submit the manuscript for publication. Once a paper is published, the contest over ownership becomes a legal one and could potentially be very costly both financially and in terms of your academic career. We realize that there are power issues here, particularly between faculty and contract staff, faculty and research students, and senior and junior faculty, that are often quite complex as they get entangled in other issues such as job security, promotion, teaching loads, administration, and so on. If, however, you feel that you are being treated unfairly then seek advice and action within your institution, resorting to legal means only where absolutely necessary.

Remember it is your responsibility as the author to acknowledge the contributions of others to the argument and analysis you are presenting, not the publisher's.

◯ Duplication

Duplication is really a form of self-copying and consists of an author publishing the same piece of text in multiple outlets without any acknowledgement of such a practice. Most journals ask whether the contents of an article are original and have not been published elsewhere. They do not want to publish work that has already been published because that work is already on the public record and available to the academic community; it also raises legal issues around copyright (see p. 36). That said, duplication is quite widely practised and in some cases is condoned, particularly where material published in an obscure or limited outlet is then submitted to an outlet with larger visibility and circulation. For example, it is not uncommon for a PhD dissertation to be reworked and submitted to a journal, where parts of the text are identical. Similarly, it is usually acceptable for material in a report with a limited circulation to be extended and reworked for a wider audience, although the editor of the journal should be notified that this is occurring and approval sought. However, it is considered unacceptable to publish large chunks of the same text in two academic journals.

○ Other practices

Other forms of plagiarism within academia, and most often associated with student assessment, are impersonation (somebody writing the piece on behalf of someone else), collusion (people working together but submitting work individually), and syndication (the reproduction and selling of work for submission) (see Carroll and Appleton, 2001; Franklyn-Stokes and Newstead, 1995). These offences similarly often carry stiff penalties, ranging from a zero mark for the assessment through to expulsion from an institution.

○ Invention and falsification

Other serious malpractices in academic publishing are invention and falsification of data and sources. As we have seen with regard to forms of plagiarism, trust is an important aspect of academic endeavour. Readers do not have full access to an author's data or their full analyses. They therefore have to trust that the data and analysis presented are real and were collected as stated. Inventing data or falsifying analysis breaks this trust and potentially has legal consequences. If discovered, an author will almost certainly face an institutional inquiry and possibly dismissal, and their academic career will be in tatters.

○ Salami publishing

Another practice that is technically not a malpractice but is often frowned upon by colleagues and university administrators, is a phenomenon known as 'salami publishing' (Luey, 2002). This consists of dividing up research into the thinnest possible slices and submitting each slice as a separate article, thus generating a number of publications. As Luey (2002) notes, while on paper this might look flattering, academic appraisals (through undertaking a literature review or more formal reviews for tenure, promotion, or grant awards) tend to assess a body of work. Thinly slicing research into slight papers will soon be noticed by peers and administrators, and its practice negatively noted. A more sensible strategy, therefore, is two or three weighty articles, as opposed to six or seven lightweight pieces.

 ## Who owns the material?

Given the growth and importance of the so-called knowledge economy, intellectual property has become a sensitive issue. The research endeavours and outputs of academics increasingly have economic worth, especially through patents and private/public consultation. It is now the case that the intellectual outputs of academics are often owned by those who funded their development, whether that be the university who paid the salary or provided the resources, or the source of funding. As a consequence, publishing material is not always straightforward. For example, when consultative research has been carried out for a private company or public body there might be restrictions on disseminating the data or findings from a study (particularly when the results might be commercially sensitive). Restrictions might prohibit some aspects of the study being published, or publication may be allowed only after a set date. Often these restrictions are detailed in the contract between the researcher and funder. It is therefore important in these cases to know, when negotiating a contract, who owns the research material produced and what this material can be used for. Once a contract has been signed, the researcher is obliged to fulfil its terms.

 ## Copyright

Copyright protects the right of the author to claim and defend a piece of work as their intellectual property, and allows them to control who can make copies of this work and how copies are made. It also allows them to sell or license the work. The author of a work holds copyright until it is transferred to another party. It is relatively standard that the publisher asks for copyright to be transferred to them on publication. With this transfer of copyright the publisher gains the right to sell the reproduction rights, translation rights, excerpt rights and the rights to adapt the piece for radio, television or film. The contract will state the recompense the author can expect if the publisher manages to sell these various rights (in other words assigning the copyright to the publisher does not mean also assigning all earning potential). The publisher will register the copyright with the relevant authorities and also work to ensure that the intellectual property is not infringed and to gain the best deal on any sales. The transfer of copyright has time limits associated with it, so that copyright reverts to the author after a specified time or if the publication goes out of print (that is, it is no longer available for purchase and there are no plans to reprint).

Seeking permission to use copyrighted material

It is illegal under copyright laws to publish previously published or copyrighted material without permission. If you wish to include excerpts of text, poetry, music, maps, photos, figures, tables, artwork, cuttings from newspapers, trademarks and so on, then you will need to seek permission from the copyright holders to do so. The obligation rests with the author, not the publisher, to seek such permissions and to provide the evidence of permission to the present publisher. Some copyright holders, particularly other publishers and archives, will charge for the reproduction of material. Again the author meets the cost unless the publisher has agreed to do so. It is very rare for a journal to agree to meet such costs.

Most publishers will provide a standardized copyright permissions form that can be used to request use of material from the original publisher. Many major publishers now offer an online facility for requesting the use of copyright material. This speeds up the process considerably. You will need to state what the material is to be used for, in what format it will be published (for example, article, paperback/hardback book), in the case of a book or report how many copies are being made and the cost of each copy, and the extent of its geographic distribution. For a book or journal article, worldwide non-exclusive rights to publish in English are generally required. In granting permission to reproduce material publishers may ask for a simple acknowledgement of the source, such as a reference citation, or they may give a specific form of words that must be used in your text. It is important that you use the exact wording stipulated and include the copyright symbol © if it is requested.

If the copyright owner cannot be located (which is often the case for older material), then the material is published with a disclaimer, which states that every effort has been made to locate the copyright holder and expresses a willingness to address copyright issues in subsequent editions should the holder be identified.

REFERENCES

Carroll, J. and Appleton, J. (2001) *Plagiarism: A Good Practice Guide.* Joint Information Systems Committee. Oxford: Oxford Brookes University.

Franklyn-Stokes, A. and Newstead, S.E. (1995) 'Undergraduate cheating: who does what and why', *Studies in Higher Education*, 20 (2): 159–72.

Luey, B. (2002) *Handbook for Academic Authors*, 4th edn. Cambridge: Cambridge University Press.

6 WRITING FOR JOURNALS AND EDITED BOOKS

Academic journals provide a specialized medium through which to disseminate research. They are usually peer-reviewed (two, three or more people read your manuscript to judge whether it is 'suitable' for publication) and the intended audience is an 'expert' group of scholars and practitioners. Each journal has a specific set of aims and objectives that differentiates it from others. Your article must be written with both the journal's aims and objectives, *and* its audience in mind. The editors of most academic journals are looking for more than a descriptive report of empirical research. Instead they want the paper to 'say' something significant and be substantiated with reasoned argument and sufficient evidence. Each journal is seeking a specific kind of content. As noted above, this can be defined by field, approach or style. An article should be tailored to fit the desired content of the journal it has been written for.

 ## Selecting a journal

It is often quite difficult to determine which journal will be the best outlet for an article, but it is perhaps a decision best made before starting to draft the text. This is because it is easier to write with a journal in mind – acknowledging from the outset its desired foci, content, style and word length – than to retro-fit the article to a journal.

In general, there are two main kinds of journals: generic and specific. The generic journals are more wide-ranging and will publish material from across the breadth of a discipline. Often they are journals of learned societies and many are tied to national organizations, although there are exceptions. Specific journals are much more focused in the remit of the material they publish, concentrating on a specific sub-field of a discipline or a particular approach or political perspective. It used to be the case that generic journals had wider circulations, readership and citation scores (see below) than specialist journals, but this is no longer always the case.

In terms of selecting a journal to send an article to, two things should be kept in mind. First, how does the journal fit with your overall publication strategy? In other words, would an article in a particular journal serve you beyond the article merely being published? Of consideration here might be the peer standing of the journal – how well it is respected and the overall perceived quality of articles published. This can be difficult to gauge, but two useful indicators of a journal's impact and popularity are its citation index score and ranking, and what colleagues have to say about it. The citation index reveals the extent to which articles within a journal are cited in other articles (note new journals do not get allocated a rating for a number of years). Publishing in a journal with a 'high' citation index can be (but is not always) important for securing tenure and promotion. The citation indices for journals are published by Thomson ISI, a private company that specializes in services to the education sector, and which can usually be accessed through academic libraries (usually under the title Web of Knowledge).

A second consideration is whether the journal serves the audience you wish to engage with? Do you want to 'talk to' a general or specialized audience; academics or practitioners; researchers from your own discipline or those from other fields? Browsing through different journals can be a useful way of identifying potential outlets. Another is to consider the journals that have published articles that you have cited.

Most researchers try to balance submissions between generic and specific journals so that differing audiences see their work. If you choose to send your paper to a specialist journal make sure it fits the aims and objectives of the journal. For example, do not send an article that does not concern gender issues to *Gender and Society* as it will meet with rejection. If in doubt ask for advice from colleagues or email the editor of the journal in advance of submitting the article and they will advise you. Whether you choose a generic or specific journal, read recent editions of the journal to get a feel for the expected content, level of scholarship and style, and also read the 'notes for contributors' (as these often outline what kind of papers the journal seeks to publish).

If you are publishing for the first time, it might be better to avoid submitting work to the top-rated publications in a field (see Chapter 2). These journals often have high rates of rejection because they have very high standards, though this is not always the case. If you are unsure whether your article is of sufficient standard for a particular journal ask for advice from colleagues who are experienced at publishing their work in journals.

General writing tips for journals

The sub-sections below provide a standard, basic structure for academic papers. There are, of course, different ways to structure articles. This sometimes depends on the content. For example, this standard structure would not generally suit a review article or one that constructs a purely theoretic argument. Alternatively, authors might devise a more imaginative way to construct and illustrate their article, although it still needs to communicate the same information and message.

The abstract

The abstract is a synopsis of (not an introduction to) the paper. It is generally around 100 words long and should detail the essence of the article (its main argument and findings) in clear and unambiguous terms so that a potential reader knows what to expect. Summarizing an entire article into so few words can be a challenging task. One way to approach it is to imagine being given 30 seconds to answer the following questions: 'So what is this paper all about and why should I read it?'

Key words

Key words, used for indexing/abstracting, are often included at the end of the abstract (check journal guidelines). Three to five specific terms are listed that will allow someone who might be interested in the article's contents to find it by searching for such terms in a database.

Introduction

The introduction is literally what it says – it introduces the substantive content of the paper. It sets the scene, providing the reader with an insight into what will follow, and details a strong rationale for the paper. It is normal for an introduction to start from the general and progress to the specific. As a consequence, it should not plunge the reader into the middle of a problem or theory. It should also never simply repeat the abstract. Booth et al. (2003: 224) suggest that an introduction should contain three elements:

- Contextualizing background (providing a general sense of what the paper is about)
- A statement of the problem (detailing the specific aspect the paper addresses and why the reader should care about this problem) and
- A response to the problem (detailing how the paper tackles the problem).

In general the introduction should be quite brief and certainly no more than a sixth of the total article length.

Literature review

It would be extremely rare for a submission to be so unique that it does not build on the work of others. A literature review is therefore a standard part of just about all articles. It details what other researchers have found, how they have theorized and researched a particular issue, and provides a context from which to illustrate how the work documented in the rest of the paper extends or advances understanding and knowledge. It also demonstrates that the author is familiar with past and present thinking and understands how their own work fits into wider intellectual debates. Given that there are word constraints on the length of an article, the literature review needs to be highly selective and specific, referring to other pieces of work most relevant to the argument being made.

Theoretical framework

This section details how the work presented in the article extends and advances previous studies; what its unique contribution is. It is usual to detail the theoretical framework or model that underpinned or arose out of the research (so that readers understand the author's ontological, epistemological and ideological view of the world), what drove the methodology and analysis, and from what perspective the analysis is being interpreted. Sometimes the literature review and theoretical framework are condensed into one section.

○ Methodology

It cannot be assumed that a reader will intuitively know how a study was undertaken. A methodology section details how the empirical material used in the article was derived. It should detail exactly how any data were generated, using what specific techniques. It should also state the numbers of cases, how they were sampled, using what rationale. If there are alternative techniques that could have been used, a justification should be provided as to why they were rejected in favour of the technique adopted. The explanation of the methodology should be sufficiently rich in detail that another researcher could replicate, and therefore test the validity of, the study. While some articles do not have a formal methodology section, they still need to state how the empirical material used to underpin any arguments was generated.

○ Analysis

An analysis section should detail how the data generated were interrogated and document the findings from the analysis. It should state clearly and unambiguously what the findings are and how they are being interpreted. Where required it should supplement the argument made with analytic evidence, whether that be statistics, tables, charts, maps, or samples of interview quotes.

○ Discussion

A discussion section takes the findings from the empirical research and links it back to the literature review and theoretical framework developed earlier. It therefore takes the argument back full circle to place the findings and argument within a broader context and details how they push forward understanding and knowledge with respect to the topic being considered. In many ways this is a crucial part of a paper as it folds together the previous sections and makes the case for the argument developed.

○ Conclusion

The conclusion brings the article to a close by summarizing the rationale and findings, reaffirming how the research advances understanding and knowledge, and outlining how future studies could build on and extend the research and argument reported.

○ References

The references section provides the reference information for papers, books, reports and so on, referred to or cited in the paper. The references listed should be complete, accurate and correctly formatted (see Chapter 4).

● Submission

Once complete, the article should be submitted as dictated in the notes for contributors printed in each issue of a journal (or available online). These notes detail how many copies of the article should be submitted and to whom. Because journals can regularly change their editors and submission policy the most recent set of notes should be consulted. A recent change in procedure for a number of journals is online submission.

Unless it is stated otherwise, give authors' names and provide contact details on a separate page (this enables blind review). If the manuscript is posted, send it flat not folded so that it can be easily photocopied if needed. Supply all tables and figures necessary.

It is common practice to include a cover letter with a submission. This simply needs to state that the article is to be considered for publication in the journal and that it has not been published elsewhere. There is no need for any long description of the paper's content or argument.

Most journals acknowledge receipt of an article, but not all. To ensure acknowledgement either send a self-addressed, pre-paid postcard or, after a short delay (to allow for postal delays and a few days when staff might be away from their desks), email the administrative office and ask whether they have received the submission.

● Referees' comments

Once an editor receives a paper, they will assess the quality of the content and writing. If the article has serious flaws – it is on a topic the journal does not concentrate on or it is very poorly written – and the editor knows from their professional experience that it will not pass successfully through the refereeing process, it will be returned to the author with some basic recommendations concerning how it needs to be altered to be considered for publication. Editors are reluctant to 'waste the time' of referees, given that they rely on their professional courtesy to read and comment on papers. If the editor feels that the article is of a basic standard, they will send it out to referees for review with guidelines as to what kind of feedback they would like (see Appendix 3). Referees are asked to judge the paper against certain criteria, such as:

- Does the paper fit the aims and brief of the journal?
- Is the topic of the paper interesting and pertinent for the journal's readership?
- Does the paper make a significant new contribution to the literature?
- Does the paper display sound scholarship?
- Is the paper clearly written and well structured?
- Is the paper of an appropriate length?

This is not to say that all journals employ the same quality thresholds, with some being more discriminating in their evaluation than others, depending on their remit. For example, some journals want to set the trend for their field and will only publish papers of the highest quality which, in the reviewers' and editor's opinion, push the bounds of current thought. These journals tend to have very high rejection rates. Other journals seek to be more inclusive, publishing articles that display high scholarship but without necessarily setting new trends.

Once an editor has received the required number of reviews, they will read the paper again in conjunction with the referees' comments, and on the basis of that reading and the views of the referees make a decision regarding publication. Most journals adopt a fourfold classification of recommendation:

- 'Accept as is'
- 'Accept with revisions' (but the paper need not be seen by a referee again)
- 'Revise and resubmit' (the revised paper will be sent out to some or all of the referees for re-evaluation) or
- 'Reject' (the paper is deemed unworthy or unsuitable for publication).

The most common deviations from this are:

- A division of the 'Accept with revisions' category into 'Accept with minor revisions' and 'Accept with major revisions'
- That the author be advised to withdraw the present paper and encouraged to submit a shorter or more focused paper or
- That the author be advised to seek publication elsewhere.

It is important to note that very few articles pass through the refereeing process without recommendations for some form of revision, even if it is just stylistic alterations. Indeed, most published papers go through several phases of revisions and editing before they are published. That said, criticism might at first be difficult to deal with. Nobody likes to be told that their work is not of a required quality.

Referees and editors, if they have done their job properly, are trying to provide constructive criticism that helps authors produce as strong a contribution as possible. As such, instead of rejecting any criticism outright, it is productive to sit back and reflect upon what the referees have said and to try to understand why they have made specific observations and recommendations. Articles that respond positively to referees' comments are always stronger submissions than the original draft submitted. Referees can give a number of reasons for revising the paper. These include:

- To strengthen an argument
- To bring in new material, ideas and thinking
- To reduce the length of the manuscript
- To strengthen the structure of the paper
- To remove repetition and redundant material
- To ensure continuity.

Revising a manuscript for resubmission

A useful strategy to aid revision is to work carefully through the referees' comments, making a list of all the suggested changes as you go. Then work through the paper, and identify the places to which these comments refer, and decide how they might be addressed. Finally, start to redraft the paper, revising and editing the text and undertaking any additional reading or analysis that might be needed. If the main problems are structural then it is important to think carefully about the 'story' being told and how best to tell it. A useful tactic might be to plot in storyboard form the 'story' and assess if the boards lead the reader smoothly through the paper.

It is important to note that not all the points and queries raised by the referees need to be addressed, especially if you disagree strongly with their assessment. However, when the revised article is re-submitted the cover letter will need to detail how the paper was revised and why specific recommendations were ignored. If the argument is compelling, and the article is now of a publishable quality, the editor will accept the paper.

 # Working papers

A working paper is generally a draft of an article intended for submission to a journal that details initial ideas about a topic or findings from a study. There are two main advantages in writing a working paper. First, they allow the author(s) to 'publish' material quickly, bypassing the time it might take for the work to pass through the reviewing and publication process of a journal. As such, working papers are often not subject to the degree of refereeing normally associated with academic journals. Secondly, they are an effective means of gathering feedback relatively quickly from colleagues and peers on the subject matter in hand, on new theories, new thoughts and so on. They are usually published as part of a series, most often sponsored by a professional organization, or a research institute or centre. However, there is nothing to stop you from initiating your own working paper series sponsored by the institution or department in which you work in order to take advantage of the ability to transfer ideas relatively quickly into a citable form.

 # Writing for a special issue

Special issues or sections in journals are becoming increasingly common. They usually bring together four to eight papers on a related topic, printing them in a single issue, and have a guest editor who organizes the issue/section in conjunction with the journal editors. Writing for a special issue/section is slightly different from an ordinary article submission. Each individual author has less say over the journal approached and they have to write to a defined brief. They therefore have to tailor their contribution in two ways: to the journal and to the brief. This obviously places certain constraints on the writing process, which have to be adhered to if the article is to be accepted and published. Another important point to note is that because the issue/section is a collection, its passage through the reviewing process and its publication date is dependent on the slowest author. Journal editors generally like all the papers to be submitted at the same time and they will not put the issue into production until the final paper has been accepted for publication. It is important then to stick to submission deadlines so as to not unnecessarily delay publication.

Writing a book review

An academic book review is a critical appraisal of a book. Interestingly, the book reviews are often one of the most-read sections of a journal because they allow researchers to keep track of what is happening in a discipline and highlight what they might or might not find useful to read. Writing a book review is now often thought of as a professional service, given that they count for little in accountancy exercises. That said, they can be very useful to undertake because they force the reviewer to read a text that might have slipped by in the maelstrom of other academic activities. Writing at least one a year is not a big chore and provides a valuable service to others.

In addition to detailing the central thesis of the book, the review should evaluate critically the strength, quality and depth of the arguments made, the style and structure of the text, and the overall significance of the book. In other words, instead of merely describing the book the reviewer expresses an opinion with regard to the value of its content. In general, the review should seek to answer the following questions:

- What is the principal focus of the book?
- What did the author set out to achieve by writing the book?
- How well has the book achieved its goals?
- What is the author's principal argument?
- Is the argument convincing and is it supported by appropriate evidence?
- Does the book significantly advance the field and, if so, how?
- Are there any significant weaknesses in the argument and evidence? What are they?
- How does the book compare with the author's previous works?
- How does the book compare with other books and articles on the same subject?

A review needs to provide a balanced but critical reflection on the content of a book. You should therefore be mindful that a review should not be:

- Patronizing, condescending or malicious

- Over-particular
- Self-promoting or
- Reactive

If you disagree with the arguments made in the book you should be careful to distinguish your viewpoint from that of the author (see Appendix 3).

Often in writing a review it is instructive to illustrate your critique by using short quotes taken from the text and/or providing reference to other relevant work. This should, however, be done in moderation. If the book is an edited collection of essays, the review should appraise critically the concept and coherence of the collection, as well as the individual essays.

Generally, book reviews are between 500 and 1000 words long, though they can be longer in specific cases. You should follow the guidelines issued by the journal.

Some journals also publish review essays in which a reviewer critically evaluates and compares two or more books that concern the same topic. Such reviews are either written by invitation or have been agreed in advance with the book review editor for the journal concerned.

Potential book reviewers are usually identified by the book review editor of a journal, who will then approach the person to see if they will write a review. Most journals are always seeking new potential reviewers and are happy to receive requests to review books.

 ## Writing an editorial/commentary

An editorial is an introduction to an edition of a journal, most typically a special issue of themed papers. It usually discusses the papers in that edition, the themes that link the papers, and highlights salient points that merit further discussion and research. It is usually written by the person who organized the special issue, or by an editor of the journal.

A commentary is a polemic piece that seeks to highlight a particular observation, argue for a particular theoretical line of thought, or call for more targeted or systematic research on a particular topic. In short, a commentary seeks to stimulate debate or action. It is usually prudent to contact the editor of the journal prior to submitting the commentary to see whether they might be interested in such an essay.

In both cases, an editorial or a commentary is generally expected to be short and concise, usually 1500–3000 words. Like ordinary articles, both editorials and commentaries require an introduction, well-structured argument, references to pertinent literature, and a conclusion. They should also be formatted in the house style of the journal concerned.

Writing a book chapter

Book chapters require the same standard of writing as journal articles, but they often differ in content and style. Many edited collections are not collections of research articles, but are more discursive pieces that explore particular issues or ideas. This does not mean that they are not empirically informed, more that the empirical material is used or examined in a different way, perhaps engaging with a particular theme or theory.

The editor of the collection will provide a brief to all authors giving guidance on the focus of the chapter, style, length and so on. This brief should be adhered to otherwise the collection as a whole can lose coherence and thus appeal. In all cases, the editor(s) will referee the chapters and make recommendations with regard to revisions. In some cases chapters will be sent out to external referees for comments. In order to provide coherence to the overall manuscript, some editors will circulate all the first drafts of chapters amongst the contributors and ask them to revise their contribution with respect to other chapters so that the entries 'talk to each other'.

In addition, time deadlines should be met. An edited book moves at the pace of the slowest author. It can be extremely frustrating to fellow authors if the publication of their contribution is delayed by several months or years because the editor is still waiting for chapters to be delivered or revised. If you are pressed for time or already over-committed and know that you will struggle to make deadlines do not agree to write a chapter. Similarly, if circumstances change, and there is the possibility that deadlines will not be met, then inform the editor so that a contingency plan can be worked out.

REFERENCES
Booth, W.C., Colomb, G.G. and Williams, J.M. (2003) *The Craft of Research*, 2nd edn. Chicago: University of Chicago Press.

7 WRITING REPORTS

As with writing journal articles, there are many elements of report writing that are essentially generic – they need to be taken into account when disseminating research in any form (for example, see Chapter 4 for general guidance on the preparation of manuscripts). In this chapter, therefore, we will focus on issues and themes that make report writing distinctive.

According to Booth (1991), a report is a formal, official statement that contains facts, is a record or documentation of findings and/or is perhaps the result of a survey or investigation. It generally lacks passion and impulse, being more restrained than other forms of dissemination, while retaining the potential for provocation (or the intention to provoke action/disturbance). A range of other terms are often used interchangeably for a report, such as memorandum, statement, account, minutes, record, paper, bulletin, briefing document, communiqué, working paper, discussion paper, case history, profile and dossier. However, each of these forms is slightly different, largely as a consequence of the context in which their development occurs.

Such diversity (based on potentially tiny differences) emphasizes the importance of knowing which form (or perhaps nuance) of 'report' is required at the outset. In particular, and helping us to further distinguish a report from the main forms of dissemination traditionally used by the academic (the discussion/working paper, the journal article . . .) Booth suggests that 'reports are not normally works of the free, unfettered, creative imagination, using a great deal of imagery, inventive vocabulary and an elaborate style'. As she adds, however, 'this does not mean that they are flat, uninteresting collections of undistinguished prose; you should use language, style and tone in an engaging way, so that the readers will quickly become (and remain) interested' (1991: 2–3). Nor does it mean, we should perhaps add, that all traditional forms of dissemination are as interesting as is implied above either!

Williams (1995) suggests that any prospective report author should be absolutely clear about their answers to the following questions:

- *What is it all about?* What are you trying to convey?
- *Why* is the report being written anyway? For what reason/purpose?
- *Who* is going to receive it? What do they want from it/you? What will happen as a result? Are they able to achieve/implement what you recommend?

Form and purpose – the intended audience

A report's length, format, structure, language and tone strongly relate to what it is that you are striving to achieve through its production, the results you wish to engender via its dissemination and the nature of its intended audience. A report is usually aimed at a wider audience than an academic journal article, so its pitch is dependent on the intended audience. For example, if the audience is largely non-academic, then the writing needs to be prepared for a lay reader, with tone, language and style being as user-friendly and straightforward as possible. Key questions to consider before composing the report concern whether the potential readership has experience of the issues and familiarity with the subject, or whether the report may need additional background information, explanation of certain terms, and so on. Alternatively, multiple versions of the final report could be produced for different audiences (perhaps with different sized fonts, different languages, and so on). However, if a clear message can be transferred from author to reader using a simple yet effective style, straightforward terminology and a lack of long-windedness, why are multiple (or more complicated) reports necessary at all?

Of course your intended audience may well be very narrow. This may particularly be the case if a particular group or organization has commissioned the report. Here you may have a very specific set of aims to work to, set by the commissioning body, that effectively leave you with limited flexibility or scope. In such cases, you simply need to produce what is required and ensure that the report serves the commissioning body's aims (rather than your own). Sometimes this can be frustrating to undertake, as you have limited flexibility and scope for manoeuvre – however, in many ways this is only to be expected and you should not enter into such arrangements without clarifying exactly what is wanted, by when, and in what form.

Form and purpose – the message

Once you have a clear idea of the intended audience, you also need to be clear about what it is that these potential readers need to be told, so that the intended purpose of the report is met. This includes being clear about the specific topic and precise message(s) you are aiming to convey. The clarity of the report message(s) can be aided by a structure that helps to frame the message(s) – perhaps through repetition at key points, perhaps by summarizing the key message(s) in an abstract or executive summary at the outset, or by using summary boxes or bullet points at the end of each section. Indeed, executive summaries are often considered to be essential in the case of long reports, where readers may not have the time or interest (however annoying this is for authors!) to read the entire report.

 # Presentation and structure

Reports are structured with respect to three main intended outcomes (Williams, 1995):

- To emphasize the main points for decision and action
- To contain plenty of facts and
- To be easy to read and navigate.

As with other forms of dissemination, the internal structure of any report should contain a beginning, a middle and an end.

Internal structure – the beginning

The 'formal' appearance of any report begins before the main text sections, with a number of potential introductory components. Booth (1991) suggests these components have the following conventional order (when they are needed):

- Title page
- Contents list
- List of illustrations
- Foreword
- Preface

- Acknowledgements
- List of abbreviations
- Summary or abstract.

It probably makes sense for some sections to come before, or after others, and their inclusion is often dependent on the length of the report, with longer reports requiring more structuring.

The title page should include the full title of the report, the name(s) of author(s), who the report is submitted to, the name and address of the publisher, and the date of publication. It can also include:

- The ISBN number (see Chapter 15)
- Notice of copyright
- Any restrictions on circulation/readership
- Details of other reports in the series (if applicable)
- Where and by whom the report was printed
- Details of the organizations that sponsored the report (or its publication/dissemination).

The report abstract and/or summary should provide the reader with clear details concerning the aims and objectives of the report, a brief methodological overview, details of key findings and subsequent conclusions, and a clear set of recommendations that emanate from these. Remember, reports are rarely read from cover to cover. Instead, readers often skim the text, focusing on sections that are most relevant to their interests and needs. The summary is therefore the key section for summarizing the overall message and findings.

The contents list allows the reader to clearly identify the main sections of the report, and where any particular themed parts of it can be found. They are particularly useful for longer reports – short reports may not need a contents list. Where one is used, however, the contents page must be accurately linked to the contents of the report. It is probably best if this part of the report is left until after the main text has been completed, with details such as page numbers only being added once the main text is not going to undergo any further changes.

Illustrations, along with tables, can be listed at the outset of the report to aid the reader. The illustrations can be numbered (1, 2, 3 . . .), or linked to the particular chapter they reside in (1.1, 1.2, 1.3 . . .) in the order they appear in the main text, and should include the exact title used in the main text.

The foreword, and/or preface can be used to draw a potential reader into the themes of the report. This can be done either by the report author(s), providing interesting details (or perhaps the rationale) behind the report (the preface), or more frequently by someone who has a background in the issues concerned, or a degree of authority/respect either in the local area or with the general themes covered (the foreword). It might also be someone who has been involved with the funding of the report.

In a similar vein, the acknowledgements give the author(s) the opportunity to thank everyone who has assisted in the production and publication of the report (in whatever form).

Any abbreviations that are drawn upon in the report should also be identified and explained in a section prior to the main text, primarily to help the reader. Whether such a section is necessary depends on who is expected to read the report, and whether the abbreviations used will be known to that readership. Similarly, a glossary of specialized terms may be necessary depending on the potential readership.

◯ Internal structure – the middle

The main text begins with the introduction. This should set the scene for the reader, be engaging and provide sufficient background details in order for the main part of the report to be fully consumed. The introduction can include information on the following (Bowden, 2000):

- Basic details concerning who commissioned the report, when and for what reason
- The terms of reference for the report author
- What resources were used and/or available to the report author
- Any limitations to the work (either during the research or writing phases)
- The sources of information used, and how these were obtained
- The methodologies employed
- The structure of the report.

Beyond the introduction, the main body of text represents the substance of the report, and its structure may also need to follow a specific pattern, dependent on the form of report, requests from funders and so on. Alternatively, you may decide that the report structure (and therefore the message) may be made clearer by utilizing a hierarchy of headings and sub-headings (perhaps numbered, perhaps drawing on different styles), and/or the numbering of individual sections or paragraphs. These stylistic 'tools' can be used to allow readers to access/identify and cross-reference specific sections of the report quickly (especially useful in meetings).

No new material should be presented in the final sections of the main text of the report, the conclusions and recommendations. The conclusions merely restate the key aspects of the report contained in previous sections and link the terms of reference to the findings. Recommendations should be derived from the conclusions and look to the future. Within the context of a report, recommendations are actionable points, next steps, or options for moving forward beyond the work presented, and should be drawn up and/or linked back to the original purpose of writing the report in the first place (the brief). They should be concise, to the point, specific and realistic (Bowden, 2000). If needed, they should be accompanied with an action plan with specific tasks, who should undertake these tasks, and an associated timetable.

◯ Internal structure – the end

Following the main text may be a number of supplementary sections. The main forms of supplementary sections are the references and suggestions for further reading (see Chapter 4), appendices and an index.

Appendices can take many forms, but they should clearly add something to the material in the main text, normally at a level of detail that goes beyond the rest of the report. They might be intended for a specialist audience (for example, statistical or technical information), relate to the methodology (for example, copies of questionnaires), or be the originals of letters and documentation referred to in the text, and so on. A key question concerns how to decide whether material you wish to include in your report is best placed in the main text, or the appendix? Perhaps the easiest answer is that if information is so important that you definitely want it to be read, place it in the main text; if the material is not essential, but will add something to the essential material, discuss it briefly and put the detail in the appendix.

Potentially the final section of the report is an index, allowing readers to delve deeply into the report and access specific topics (that are hidden by the more general contents page at the outset of the report); in fact it may well be more likely that readers will work from the index backwards, than from the contents forwards! Compilation of an index is a joyless, time-consuming task. As a first stage, you should identify what you consider to be key topics within the report, and where they occur. These should then be arranged in order, with sub-terms included beneath the main/key term. At a later stage links can be made between entries as a form of cross-referencing.

Production and dissemination

The final main consideration of report writing concerns production and dissemination. There are fewer constraints concerning the design and physical presentation of reports than academic journal publications, where the journal article submission rubric is often fairly formal. However, this does not necessarily mean anything goes – as noted above, many aspects of report production are delimited by the eventual purpose of the report. Despite this, however, your report always needs to be accessible, with a clear and direct message (meaning that word length should probably not be excessive), and a welcoming layout (with clear sections and headings, readable sized font, large margins, uncrowded line-spacing, etc.). Pictures and/or diagrams are particularly useful in breaking up large expanses of text, and catching the eye of any potential reader. If a report has a general readership (rather than being produced for a select group who do not necessarily need to be encouraged to read it) then a bright or attractive cover may induce potential readers to look closer. Production of an executive summary (or similar) can also stimulate potential readers.

A commercial publisher rarely produces reports, even if they are being produced for an agency. Rather the authors become much more involved in the production process and this brings them into the territory of self-publication (see Chapter 15). If the funding is available, most of the jobs can be farmed out to specialists (designers, typesetters, printers, binders) and so on, but rather than the publisher's production editor doing this work, the authors will have to manage the project. This can be a costly exercise both in terms of time and money. Producing a timetable and obtaining full costings in advance of starting the production phase can ensure a relatively smooth passage through production.

Many universities have their own 'reprographics' and/or design services departments capable of producing reasonably sized reports and publications in-house. This means that everything from the initial desktop design through to printing and binding is conducted (almost) under one roof, or at least normally on the same site. This can be highly advantageous in that it means you should probably end up dealing with only one person, potentially allowing you to (feel as if you) have more control over the process. At its simplest this process entails answering the designer's questions about the type of publication style, form and so on you require, showing them any examples you would like them to draw inspiration from, providing them with the basic unformatted text (and/or any visual elements you need included) and letting them get on with it! They will then do what they do best, and return your text in draft form for you to amend as necessary and return. There may be subsequent revisions until you are happy that the product is finished. When you are fully satisfied with every aspect of the draft product, you will be asked to sign the job off, and it will then enter the printing stage.

Obviously your report can be as glossy, eye-catching and colourful as you would like, as long as you have the resources to produce it. When any work is being tendered for, therefore, it is always worth gathering quotes about the production of a notional report at the end of the project. All too often fascinating research is drained of life by its dissemination in a staid, uninspiring, unimaginative format and style, or its impact restrained by a lack of funding for adequate dissemination.

If you have a key future date by which you require your report to be ready then you should obviously work backwards from there once the estimated design and production schedule is notified to you, and give yourself plenty of additional time for those unexpected events or last minute changes/additions and problems. If, on the other hand, you have the luxury of being able to identify publication after the production process is complete, a somewhat less stressful period may occur instead.

Finally, your report can also be accompanied by an official 'launch', again helping to maximize exposure for the document (and you as its author). This can be as formal or informal as necessary – it can include refreshments, events and activities, or it can be a simple presentation of key findings to those who need to know. Whatever the type of event, it should be well organized, with relevant supporting information coordinated through an official press release (to minimize the chance of the message of your report getting lost – see Chapter 9).

REFERENCES

Booth, P.F. (1991) *Report Writing*, 2nd edn. Huntingdon: Elm Publications.

Bowden, J. (2000) *Writing a Report*. Oxford: How To Books.

Williams, K. (1995) *Writing Reports*. Oxford: The Oxford Centre for Staff Development.

8 Publishing on the Internet

The Internet is increasingly becoming a popular medium for disseminating and discussing research. The Internet consists of millions of interlinked computers bound together through telecommunications technologies (copper, coaxial and glass cables, as well as radio and microwaves). Each linked computer resides within a nested hierarchy of networks, from its local area, to its service provider, to regional, national and international telecommunication networks. Consequently, the Internet is literally a network of networks that link together computers and the information and services they store globally. The media that the Internet supports are diverse, varying in sophistication and immediacy. Users can browse information stored on other computers, exchange electronic mail, participate in discussion groups on a variety of topics, transfer files, search databases, take part in real-time conferences and games, explore virtual worlds (both textual and visual), run software on distant computers, and buy goods and services (see Dodge and Kitchin, 2000). While all of these media are the focus of research or used to conduct research, the most common media for disseminating research are mailing lists, bulletin boards and websites.

Mailing lists and bulletin boards

Mailing lists are centralized, and in some cases monitored, forums for allowing a number of individuals to converse or swap information via email on specific topics. Every email message sent to the list is redistributed to all the other subscribers who then have the opportunity to respond. There are thousands of academic mailing lists that provide forums for discussing just about every kind of research topic, or for advertising events such as conferences (see, for example, http://www.jiscmail.ac.uk/). An alternative to mailing lists is provided by bulletin boards. Bulletin boards offer access to a number of functions. These include newslists and chat facilities. Newslists act like 'real-world' bulletin boards and are centralized places to post and read mail. Users can periodically check the board for messages, which are organized under subject headings. Within each subject there are normally several threads of conversation. Users can choose whether to 'un-pin' a message, read it and reply. As such, the system works in the opposite way to mailing lists. Whereas all mail on a mailing list is posted to all members of the list, all users of a bulletin board must go to the board to check for mail. Usenet is by far the largest collection of newslists, with literally thousands of groups discussing all manner of topics (see http://groups.google.com/ or http://www.usenet.org.uk/).

Both mailing lists and bulletin boards provide relatively informal environments in which to discuss or promote research. Neither medium is formally refereed, although some lists are moderated for potentially offensive emails, commercial spam, and irrelevant content *vis-à-vis* the focus of the list. Neither medium is the place to submit full articles or substantive written pieces. Instead submissions should be aimed at stimulating debate and discussion, be replies to previously posted mails, or be informative, letting other list members know about a forthcoming conference, event, launch of a report or book or new website, and so on. As a consequence, lists and boards can be extremely useful media for finding out the latest ideas and trends, and also what events are happening. It is important to remember that a reply to a mail from a list will often go to the whole list, not just your intended recipient. As a result, you should make sure that you check the recipient return line before sending any personal views or details.

 ## Websites

Websites are the visual interface to the World Wide Web (WWW). A website is a collection of multimedia data (mostly text and static graphics but also sound, animation and movie clips) which are stored as hypermedia 'pages' (documents that contain links to other pages of information). Usually a website will consist of several interlinked 'pages'. By clicking the mouse cursor on a link (usually highlighted text or a graphical icon) the user is transported between pages. As such, the WWW provides a powerful medium in which to explore related subjects, allowing users to easily 'jump' between, and search for, other relevant documents, without concern for their specific location. In addition to displaying hypermedia documents, the introduction of Java and the use of other plug-in applications now mean that programs can be run and downloaded across the Web. Websites are increasingly being used both to conduct research (by providing access to libraries and public and private information) and to disseminate research. With regard to the latter, there are a number of different websites through which research is disseminated.

Institutional and project sites

A website or blog provides the opportunity to create a window on the work of an institute, research team or individual researcher and the work that they do. They are relatively inexpensive, particularly when compared to printed media and associated postage costs, easy for anyone with access to the Internet to find and browse, can be updated on demand, and facilitate correspondence. The website can be used to provide information on specific projects, access to working papers or on-going results, details on research staff, and so on. A blog is an online diary (or log) of observations and opinions. A well-constructed website that provides useful information to browsers is a valuable networking and marketing tool, and lets people know about research being undertaken well ahead of articles appearing in peer-review journals.

Online journals

Most online journals are the equivalent to print journals in terms of their procedures and outputs but they only exist in a virtual form. In other words, authors submit their articles that are then peer-reviewed, before a decision is made as to whether to publish. Once an article is accepted for publication it is generally placed into an issue, with the issue then published in one go rather than the article being published as soon as it is correctly formatted. The benefit of online publication is that the time an article waits in a queue for publication can be substantially reduced as there are often no restrictions on the number of issues in a year (as with print media). In addition, the article has a very large potential audience, particularly if the journal does not require a subscription fee and is therefore freely available (most are free unless they are commercial ventures).

As with many new media until proven and established, many university administrators have placed a question mark over the quality and perceived worth of online journals. This is because online journals differ from traditional tried and trusted paper-based journals in that an established publisher does not assure their quality, they are mostly free and anyone can start such a journal. Moreover, they rarely appear in the ISI indexes. Research account-ancy exercises thus remain cautious as to how to judge the worth of online articles and this has made some authors wary of publishing their work through this medium. That said, their popularity and reputation is growing and many traditional journals are publishing issues simultaneously in print and online (albeit for a subscription fee). It certainly seems the case that the future is virtual dissemination rather than paper-based production.

○ Working paper repositories

Given how long peer-review publication takes, it is increasingly common in some disciplines for early drafts of submitted papers to be published as online working papers ensuring that the findings and ideas are circulated when they are new and fresh. These are often published as part of a depart-mental or institutional series, but can also be distributed through large working paper repositories. An example from economics is the Repec web-site (Research Papers in Economics) that provides access to thousands of working papers and articles (http://repec.org/).

○ E-books

An e-book is the same as a printed book but is published online. There are two basic kinds, those that are digital, downloadable versions of printed books (see www.ebooks.com) and those that are entirely virtual and have no distributed, printed counterpart (see Fuller and Kitchin 2004 for an example). The latter are relatively rare for academic publishing, but it is a means of publication increasingly being explored, especially in light of printed publishing trends. E-books can be published on an individual or institutional research site or as part of an coordinated e-book series or site or through a commercial site (see http://www.ebooksnbytes.com/ for advice and links). In the latter case, the e-publisher will sell the book online, split-ting the profits with the author. The advantages of an e-book are that the author retains much fuller control of the content, it is cheap and relatively easy to implement, the content can be updated and expanded over time, novel additions such as animations, movies and sound files can be embed-ded in the text, and the manuscript has a very wide potential audience.

⦿ Commercial and product sites

The Internet also opens up the potential to exploit research commercially (or at least to cover some of the costs). A commercial or product website offers some of the outputs of research, such as reports and software, for sale. This requires investment in payment processing software and expert commercial and computing advice to ensure safe and secure payments.

Issues to consider

General issues related to self-publishing are discussed see Chapter 15; however there is a number of issues specific to e-publishing of which you should be aware.

⦿ Ownership

Webspace can either be owned by a company or institution or can be purchased individually. If neither you, nor your institution own the site on which you are publishing, you should ascertain who 'owns' the published material, its copyright status, and what your rights are *vis-à-vis* updating the material if required. If the website *is* owned by the university or institution for which you work, it is increasingly the case that any intellectual ideas and research presented on the site are considered the intellectual property of the institution. If you want your own site, it is relatively easy and cheap to buy a domain name and get a website hosted and there are a plethora of companies that offer registration and hosting services (e.g. register.com). In effect, you 'rent' the domain name for a set number of years and you should be careful to renew your subscription so that you do not lose the domain name.

⦿ Copyright

Just as with print media, there are copyright obligations and permission is needed to put other people's or institutions' data online (see Chapter 5). Failure to obtain such permissions may well result in legal action.

For information on protecting the copyright of self-published material see Chapter 15.

○ Contracts

It is standard practice for there to be a contract between author and publisher for paper-based publications. This contract protects the interests of both author and publisher and places an obligation on both to fulfil their respective roles and duties. While becoming more common, especially for those sites run on a commercial or professional basis, it is not standard practice that authors of material online receive and are protected by a publishing contract. Instead, much of the relationship is based on trust. This is fine if everything works out, but it can be very problematic if the relationship between author and publisher breaks down. Although the author still retains right of ownership and copyright, it can be difficult to remove or censor material from the Web, and legal proceedings could be expensive. Our advice is to only allow others to publish your material online if you believe them to professional and reputable. If in doubt, ask for a contract that states the obligations of both author and online publisher.

○ Security

The Internet has varying degrees of security. Generally anybody who has access to a website can view and download all the material that is presented unless there are some security measures that limit user access. Implementing security might mean only permitting users to view material if they type in the correct username or password, or it might be restricting access to computers with a certain IP (network) address. If you want to place limited access material online for purposes of sharing it with colleagues then our suggestion is to consult with the hosts of your webspace for advice.

○ Design and access

An effective website is one that looks professionally produced and is well organized and structured, allowing users to find the information they require. The design does not have to include fancy animations and graphics to communicate effectively. In fact, such additions can hamper the access of those who do not have high-speed access to the Internet and limit the access of the site to disabled people, especially those who are visually impaired. To ensure that a website is accessible to the most number of people and complies with accessibility guidelines visit http://bobby.watchfire.com/bobby/html/en/index.jsp (which conducts a free test and reveals how the site should be modified). A professional company will help with all of these issues for a fee, but if this is not feasible and the website is going to be 'home-made' then consult handbooks that will give practical advice. A well-made website will serve you much better than one that is poorly designed and structured.

○ Perceived quality and worth

As noted above, there are still a few hang-ups with respect to the perceived quality and academic worth of online publications. This is particularly so with respect to research accountancy exercises. There is no doubt though that the situation is changing as researchers become familiar with the new media and come to understand its benefits with regard to distribution and flexibility of formats. If you need a piece of written work to 'count' for tenure or a research accountancy exercise, our advice is to check with those doing the assessing as to how they view e-publishing. In general, however, such ventures will probably be the future of research publishing and should be supported and viewed positively.

REFERENCES

Dodge, M. and Kitchin, R. (2000) *Mapping Cyberspace*. London: Routledge.

Fuller, D. and Kitchin, R. (eds) (2004) *Radical Theory, Critical Praxis: Making a Difference Beyond the Academy?* Praxis E-Press. http://www.praxis-epress.org/rtcp/contents.html

9 DISSEMINATION THROUGH POPULAR MEDIA

If you feel that your work has particular salience or want to reach a wider audience then one you might want to consider publicizing your research through popular media. There are various forms that such media can take, from newspapers and magazines of varying types and styles, through to more immediate and potentially anxiety-inducing forms such as radio and television. Perhaps the main reason why you might want to utilize these forms is to make knowledge(s) available beyond the traditional halls of academia. In part this relates to a perceived change in the status of academics from 'legislators' to 'interpreters' (Bauman, 1987), and a not-unrelated desire to make a difference 'beyond the academy' by reaching out to, and working with other groups and individuals. Whatever the reasoning, use of such forms necessitates awareness of a potentially whole new set of issues to those that arise from sources traditionally utilized by academics.

 ## Newspapers

Local newspapers and local/regional radio/television are 'content hungry' and are constantly on the look out for stories, including stories related to research. This does not mean that they will respond to every press release, but they will be potentially interested in a 'newsworthy' story such as the launch of a new report or a scientific breakthrough. If the story has wider appeal it will be picked up the national press, as they often look to local and regional presses for material. That said, press releases should only be utilized as part of a broader strategy of dissemination – if they are sent too often, or are poorly constructed, they will hinder your attempts to hit the headlines rather than help.

If you want to try to attract newspaper coverage, the first step is to prepare a press release (see Box 9.1). If your university has media relations staff they will be able to help with drafting a press release and suggesting potential journalists to contact.

Box 9.1 Preparing a Press Release

- Press releases should be word-processed and double-spaced. They should be concise – no more than two pages, and preferably only one page.
- The story should be written for a reading age of 12–14 years old (see next section).
- Make sure that the date of release is stated clearly at the top, along with full contact details.
- Next type in capital letters a working title. This title should provide the essence of the story and is designed to capture an editor's attention (in other words, it should be a bold statement).
- Start by asking yourself a question: 'How are people going to relate to this and will they be able to connect?'.
- The first paragraph of your press release should contain all the salient elements of your story. It must contain the hook – this paragraph will decide if the editor reads on. Answer the six basic questions of journalism: who, what, when, where, why, how. If possible use a common question (e.g., 'Have you ever wondered . . .') or an anecdote (e.g., 'Joe Bloggs was often . . .').
- The body of the text should be written with the most important information and quotes first.
- At the end of the release, sum up the essence of your argument or findings and indicate from whom further information is available (provide phone and fax numbers and an email address).
- If you want to enclose photographs, figures or tables, do so using a paper clip (not staples or tape). They must be of sufficient quality to reproduce.
- Target the papers most likely to be interested in your story. Generally, national papers will not be interested in local news.
- Make sure you know the story deadline of weekly and daily newspapers so that you can ensure that your news will arrive in time for publication.

cont.

- Make sure you indicate an embargo if you do not want the story covered until after a certain date.
- When complete, type '# # #' at the bottom of the page (a way of saying 'the end').

Adapted from http://www.alphagalileo.org/ and http://www.search engines.com/ (see for more detail). For links to over 17,000 newspapers and news sources see http://www.abyznewslinks.com

If you are approached by a newspaper

If a newspaper contacts you about a possible story based on your work, you need to think carefully how to proceed. If their intended story is a critique of your research, it is usually best to try to cooperate in some way – especially if they are going to run the story regardless. If your university has media relations staff, contact them for help. If the press ring you up without warning, it is useful to ask what it is they are interested in, say that you are busy, but that you will ring them back in 20 minutes. This gives you time to collect your thoughts and to think about what you want to say. One way to try to control what is written is to offer to draft a piece yourself. Journalists will often take up this offer as they are usually short of time and trying to meet deadlines.

Writing for newspapers

According to Hicks et al. (1999: 9), journalism 'is informal rather than formal; active rather than passive; a temporary, inconclusive, ad hoc, interim reaction rather than a definitive measured statement . . . Journalism may be factual or polemical, universal or personal, laconic or ornate, serious or comic, but on top of the obvious mix of information and entertainment its stock in trade is shock, surprise, contrast.' As such, writing for newspapers entails translating your message into what former journalist Nicholas Bagnall (1993: 2) terms 'newspaper language':

> The professional spokesperson, the white-collar worker with a stake in his firm, the landowner, the political careerist, the specialist jealous of her expertise, all use language as a shield to protect their particular interests. Politicians may use words which sound grand but have no actual meaning. Experts use obscure words and phrases to show that only they and their colleagues can

understand the point at issue . . . The journalist is the complete opposite. His or her task is to break down the shield and to disclose what others may be trying to conceal . . . Immediate clarity, then, is the aim. Clarity, and directness'

Newspaper language is, therefore, much closer to the spoken word than is business or academic language, a trend exacerbated in recent years by the rise in the dissemination of news by live announcers/broadcasters. In essence, or perhaps that should be, in short, this means purging 'one's copy of words which sound pedantic and oratorical, when they have perfectly good equivalents in ordinary speech' (1993: 4). Bagnall illustrates this point with a range of words and their pedantic equivalents, including the following:

Answer	(respond)
Begin	(commence)
End	(conclude, terminate)
Find out	(ascertain)
Hurry	(expedite)
Lit	(illuminated)
Tell	(inform, apprise, acquaint, narrate)
Was bruised	(suffered contusions)

Bagnall's point is simple – when writing for newspapers '[w]e shouldn't be thinking of the elaborate one first' (1993: 7).

This does not mean, however, that such elaborate words should never be used. Sometimes they are necessary, or are simply more expressive. However, they should be avoided when the shorter alternative is what is meant, and a more elaborate one has its own nuance/purpose; the elaborate word is a luxury and/or simply unnecessary.

Another point to bear in mind concerns the use (or otherwise) of jargon. Again Bagnall cautions against merely dispensing with the use of jargon, suggesting instead that it should not be used 'just to show off', and where it is used, it should be explained, as it can add to the authenticity of any piece. Hicks et al. (1999: 9) suggest that 'journalists are interpreters between specialist sources and the general public, translators of scientific jargon into plain English, scourges of obfuscation, mystification, misinformation. Or they should be.'

Of course, all of these comments need to take account of the variety of forms of newspaper press, with the different forms often necessitating different styles of newspaper language. While academics might claim that it is the more formal 'broadsheets' that are likely to take the most interest in their work rather than the 'red tops' or tabloids, probably the most frequently used form of press is the local newspaper, which, in our experience, seems to relate most closely to populist tabloids rather than the 'serious' broadsheets.

In a similar fashion to the production of effective press releases, writing for newspapers should follow a clear structure, answering in turn who, what, how, where, when and why (Hicks et al., 1999). Further, the structure of writing can often be likened to the shape of a pyramid, where the top represents the first line – something short and concise that will grab the reader's attention, make sense, and also convey the main aspects of the news/feature – with detail increasing as the article progresses. The aim is to allow the reader to stop reading when their curiosity is satisfied without missing anything important (Hicks et al., 1999). Here, Bagnall (1993) makes reference to the 'soup test' – being able to recount the essence of a story before your dinner partner moves their spoon for the next mouthful!

 # Magazines

Magazines are more open to offers of features, rather than simply news stories. Like newspapers, they have to fill issues on a regular basis, and if they think your work is topical they will gladly accept a piece for publication. Clearly, there is a huge range of magazines available for potential submissions. These range from the glossy consumer magazines (with circulation figures in their millions) through to a range of trade and business magazines of varying scope and breadth of interest. Whether populist or not, each usually incorporates a range of different sections and (potential) article/feature types within any single issue.

As such, there is a large degree of choice available to the budding magazine feature writer as to where to submit their work. Evidence suggests (see Dick, 1996) that article acceptance rates/sales of submissions are increased by initially focusing on the identification of a relevant market (or magazine type at least, if not the specific magazine), with the actual idea for an article coming later. Like academic journal writing, operating in this way will also make it easier to tailor your submission to the relevant niche at the outset, rather than editing and re-slanting afterwards.

Unless you have already developed a relationship in some form with a magazine editor, it is probably advisable to contact the editor prior to drafting a submission to see if they are interested. At this point you can also confirm details such as the lead-in time until publication, the correct length of submission, style and format, and if they require images or other illustrative material. It normally takes between four and eight months for an article to appear in a well-established monthly magazine. For a weekly magazine the time-scale is obviously reduced, but the principle is the same – allow plenty of time and plan ahead if you wish to see your work in print at any specific time, or to coincide with a particular event.

As with writing for newspapers, it is again crucial to remember that, in general terms, a magazine article is very different in style from an academic paper – it needs to catch a reader's attention quickly, state the main arguments or findings clearly and early in the article, and be pitched at the right level for the audience (for example, is the magazine specialist or generalist in nature?). Many magazines pay for contributions and you should be careful to negotiate any fee at the outset of the assignment (in most cases there will be standard fees, usually calculated on the number of pages an article fills).

 ## Radio and television

It is (nearly) always flattering to receive a phone call from a local (or possibly national) radio or television station asking if you would be willing to contribute your views to one of their shows, or give a brief interview for the news team. Somehow, you need to balance feeling good that your work has received recognition and is obviously considered to be interesting, if not groundbreaking, with the need to be calm, controlled and clinical in dealing with the task ahead.

As with contact from newspaper journalists, the best response to a 'cold call' about an aspect of your work (or other issue) is to ask if you can return their call after a short period of time. Again this is to allow you some time to collect your thoughts, gather together relevant documents or information, and so on. This is especially important if your words are going to be recorded there and then (normally for radio) via the telephone, rather than having an initial discussion that might lead to a contribution at a later time/date. If this does happen, be sure to find out as much as you can about the programme you will be 'appearing' on, why the topic (and therefore your work) is of interest, what questions or issues the interviewer wants to explore, and what angle the interviewer or programme will be taking. It would also be helpful to find out who the audience will be. Then take your 'time out', gather relevant materials to help you, and call them back.

In basic terms you need to identify what the key points are that you wish to get across to the audience, and how best to convey them. Live broadcasts in particular are always unpredictable (no matter what you are told you will be talking about beforehand), and you want to avoid having to think 'on the hoof' as much as possible. Try to have every avenue covered in terms of what may be thrown at you – alternatively, take a leaf from any seasoned politician and reply to whatever rogue question is being asked with your pre-identified key points ('Well I'm not sure about that, but what I can tell you is a . . . b . . . c . . .').

Obviously if the initial call is an attempt by the journalist or researcher to identify whether your work or views are interesting, and you pass this first hurdle, you may be asked to contribute your views at a later date. This is much less stressful (initially at least), and allows you far more time to gather the relevant information necessary to ensure you are well prepared.

When the time comes, you are probably best to avoid 'hedging', or sitting on the fence – most broadcasters prefer interviewees with something interesting or possibly controversial to say. This is not to suggest that you should be deliberately confrontational or contentious for the sake of it, just that the broadcasters will prefer those who 'give good copy'. Whatever the case, you should speak clearly and distinctly, to the level of the audience. If your work makes use of, or is embedded in technical terms, or jargon, be sure to explain these terms in a non-patronizing way. The final point is to be prepared for your contribution to be much shorter than you would either like, or expect. This is particularly the case if you are contributing to an item in a newscast, or feature, as these (particularly the former) tend to be based around short, sharp 'sound-bites' rather than well-constructed, reasoned debate. This was certainly brought home to us when one of us was awoken (on the launch day of a major piece of work) by his own voice coming from the radio, and a five-second 'summary' of the views he had recounted at some length to a researcher the previous day!

Contributing to a television programme requires awareness of similar issues to contributing to radio, but is obviously rather more 'performance'-related due to the fact that you will be seen, not just heard, by any number of other people. As such, your preparation should include the same enquiries as for appearing on the radio, alongside a focus on most aspects concerned with giving a 'presentation' (see Chapter 19).

The one respite you might have here is that as long as you are not being broadcast live, you have the potential for multiple 'takes' if things go particularly badly! Appearing on television can certainly be a challenging task – but it can also be fun. At the very least it may provide experiences that are out of the ordinary, and/or contribute to your '15 minutes of fame', as you attempt to concentrate on your interviewer while the cameraman is performing all sorts of acrobatics to get that 'arty' shot, or have to converse with an interviewer without being able to see them, while millions of viewers can see you. Prepare well and remember that you almost certainly know a lot more about the topic than the interviewer.

REFERENCES

Bagnall, N. (1993) *Newspaper Language*. Oxford: Focal Press.

Bauman, Z. (1987) *Legislators and Interpreters: On Modernity, Postmodernity, and the Intellectuals*. Cambridge: Polity Press.

Dick, J. (1996) *Writing for Magazines*. London: A&C Black.

Hicks, W., Adams, S. and Gilbert, H. (1999) *Writing for Journalists*. London: Routledge.

10 TYPES OF BOOKS AND SELECTING A PUBLISHER

Writing a book is a major undertaking. In general, it takes between one and two years to complete a manuscript, even if it is an edited collection, and in many cases takes substantially longer. Careful decisions therefore need to be taken with regard to the type of book you wish to write and who would be the best publisher. It is probably wise to seek a publisher before starting work to ensure that such efforts are not in vain. This can be quite a challenge, especially since the nature of academic book publishing has changed significantly over the past twenty years. This is largely a function of consolidation in the publishing industry, so that just a few international companies dominate the sector. These companies are driven by turnover and have rationalized their publishing lists to try to maximize their profits. Other smaller publishers have to some extent filled the specialist niches left, but the size of their lists does not often match those that were cut by larger publishers. What this means is that it is increasingly difficult to publish some kinds of books, especially with the larger, more established publishers.

In general two kinds of books have suffered most, the research monograph and edited texts. Both are seen as having small, niche markets. Instead publishers are seeking more pedagogic texts that will ensure sales to students as well as academics, and texts that might have appeal across disciplines. In addition, popular science and social science books have also grown in popularity, fuelled by lay reader demand. As a result, commissioning editors are reluctant to commission texts that they do not believe will have wide market appeal. That said, this should not put you off writing a book, though it obviously shapes the context in which such an endeavour occurs.

What type of book for what type of audience?

Prospective authors usually have a pretty good idea as to the type of book they want to write and who they anticipate will buy and read the text. That given, there is no harm in thinking about the various types of book possible, and how they suit different objectives.

Books take one of two principal forms, authored and edited. Authored books are texts whose entirety has been drafted by a single person or team. Edited books are manuscripts where each chapter is written by a different contributor, commissioned, directed and edited by an editor or a team of editors. In both cases there are a variety of different forms that can be utilized for disseminating research and ideas, each of which targets a different audience and consumer.

A research monograph is a specialist text aimed at fellow researchers. It is usually narrow in scope and technically and theoretically sophisticated. As a consequence, the audience is usually fairly small, limited to other academics. Only a few of these academics are likely to buy the book directly and the main consumers are often university libraries. Given the specialist audience, the print run can be very small (500–1000 copies) and the price per copy high (to ensure a profit from limited sales). As libraries are principal purchasers, these books are often produced in hardback form only (hardbacks last longer than paperbacks if being used by multiple readers). To ensure a paperback version the author(s) must convince the publisher that there is a potentially large target market beyond libraries, for example using their past sales record as evidence, or making the case that the book will sell across disciplines, to specialist lay or industry readers, or to advanced students.

A 'popular' monograph is a text that is still quite specialized in nature but is written in a manner that is clear to a part- or non-specialist audience. It most usually takes the form of a 'popular science', coffee table, or generalist, non-fiction text (for example, history, politics, biography). It aims to present technical or sophisticated analysis in a straightforward, non-complex manner. Most academics would probably like to think that they either already are, or could readily mutate into, the authors of such accessible texts, as public intellectuals, able to explain the ideas and writing of academia and communicate them clearly and effectively to a lay audience. In reality, communicating specialist material in a non-specialist way, clearly explaining terms and arguments, is a skill. It requires an appreciation that non-specialist readers do not have the benefit of certain knowledges, are not used to thinking in an 'academic manner', and that the text needs to be lively and engaging (not dry and dull, as much academic writing is, or at the very least, might be perceived to be). Because such a text is aimed at a larger market, and will involve a larger print run and a lower price, a publisher will need to be confident that the text will be written and presented in a manner that will generate sales. As a result, publishers can be quite cautious at commissioning academics to write such texts, often preferring journalists or professional writers. Securing a contract will necessitate demonstrating a strong commercial idea, a good writing style, and the willingness to stick to the brief.

A *specialist-edited collection* is a book containing a number of chapters by different authors on a particular theme. They usually arise out of conferences or symposia and draw together a number of related papers. The strength of such an approach is that it brings together a range of expertises, knowledges and perspectives that a single author is unlikely to possess. The content of chapters can vary, being determined by the chapter authors, by the collection editor, or as compromise between authors and editor. If the chapter is commissioned, the author is given a brief and a template to work to. The consumers of specialist-edited collections are almost exclusively academic libraries. Given their small circulation and marginal profits, many publishers are now becoming cautious about commissioning such texts, especially international, commercial publishers. This is not to say that no such books are commissioned. However, in order to interest a publisher the proposal will need a strong rationale and will have to make a convincing case that a ready market exists. If a publisher cannot be found, the collection could be offered to a journal as a possible special issue or published on-line as an e-book (see Chapter 8).

A *handbook* is a pedagogic text aimed at a non-student audience, whether that be specialist or non-specialist in nature. A successful handbook needs to combine the qualities of a popular monograph and a textbook. That is, it must have wide, general appeal, be written for a part- or non-specialist audience, and be pedagogically useful.

A *festschrift* is a particular kind of edited text that celebrates the life of a scholar. Such works are usually presented to the academic on retirement. A publisher is unlikely to be interested in such a text unless the scholar was very well known and respected or a subvention is forthcoming to defray some production costs (see p. 94).

A *textbook* is a pedagogic text aimed at a student audience. Its primary purpose is to help students learn material appropriate to a course. There are usually several textbooks devoted to any one topic on the market at any one time. Publishers will only be interested in a new textbook idea if it fills a niche not already occupied or if it is sufficiently novel to challenge established texts. Given how competitive and lucrative the textbook market is, however, they will always be willing to evaluate a proposal. For the textbook to succeed, the content and sophistication of the text needs to be pitched at an appropriate level for the intended students. In other words, textbooks should be introductory, intermediate or advanced in nature and it is important that this level is maintained throughout the text. Textbook sales are often dependent on staff recommendations to students. If the text covers inappropriate or out-dated material, is pitched at the wrong level, or covers the same ground as the books already used, the likelihood is that it will not be adopted.

An edited textbook is a pedagogic text where each chapter is produced by a different author. Such texts are gaining popularity amongst publishers, especially as it is becoming more difficult to persuade many academics to write textbooks given their relative lack of worth in research accountancy exercises (a single chapter is more manageable), the time such a venture takes, and the many other commitments that need to be offset. As with edited collections *per se*, it will need very strong editorship (see Chapter 14). Chapters will have to be commissioned, with authors given a specific brief with regards to content, structure and level. Authors will need to be held to this brief, being asked to revise the text if it strays too far from what is required.

A dictionary or encyclopaedia is a particular kind of edited collection, usually very broad (for example, disciplinary) in scope. An academic dictionary provides definitions of key concepts, perhaps elaborating how the meaning and operation of each concept has developed over time and supplies links to key readings. An encyclopaedia similarly defines and explains concepts, but usually includes other information relevant to a field, such as biographies of key individuals, key places or networks, theoretical approaches, key debates, and so on. Both dictionaries and encyclopaedias are organizationally complex, involving many authors, and extremely expensive to produce. Given the size and cost of the project and the need for extensive networks to generate entries, it would be extremely rare for a publisher to commission anybody but a senior academic within a field to be an editor.

A reader is an edited text that brings together a number of previously published papers that focus on a particular topic. The goal is to provide students with a single volume that contains all the (perceived) essential, advanced readings that might be expected to accompany a module. They tend to be quite popular in North America where there has been a ready tradition of course leaders providing photocopies of articles in a bound form to students. A successful reader is a text that contains articles that would be used for supplementary readings across courses on the same topic, regardless of course leader. Generally publishers prefer a senior academic to compile a reader, but will consider a more junior scholar if the rationale of the proposal is compelling.

Do you need an agent?

In general, most researchers do not employ an agent to secure a book contract, instead dealing directly with commissioning editors. An agent might, however, be useful if you are seeking to publish a text aimed at a general, rather than academic, audience – for example a popular science or general history text. An agent might also be useful if you have ambitions to widen the work beyond a text, for example as a radio or television documentary. In these cases, agents will use their contacts and networks to sound out prospective publishers or documentary-makers and then broker any deal. Cultivating these networks independently might be quite difficult.

It is important to remember that an agent is commercially oriented – if your project does not make money then nor do they. Agents are therefore looking for projects that will be commercially successful. It follows that in pitching your idea to an agent you must be able to explain clearly and convincingly, using examples where possible, why large numbers of the general public will be interested in your research or thesis. If the agent is not convinced of a manuscript's commercial potential they will decline representation.

It is very difficult to judge an agent by their entry in a trade book such as *The Writers' Handbook* (Turner, 2004). If possible try to solicit a personal recommendation. Otherwise, judge on the basis of what authors and material they presently represent. Most agents tend to specialize in particular topics and there is little point contacting an agent who does not cater for your field.

Selecting a publisher

The first step in choosing a publisher is to narrow down the field to those that publish the kind of book you wish to produce (monograph, textbook, etc.). The second step is to study the list of books presently published by each press, discarding those that do not have a track record of publishing work in your specialty. The third step is to assess the remaining publishers and narrow them down to one or two you might approach. This assessment is best done by evaluating: their reputation in terms of their production, marketing and distribution (through collecting colleagues' views and looking at the catalogues); the nature of their lists; and who writes for them. Finally, informally approach the relevant commissioning editors of your shortlist either by phone or email (their details will usually be on the publisher's website) or by visiting the book stands at a major conference (which many publishers attend to sell their books and journals and meet with their authors). The commissioning editor will listen to your initial pitch and give you an indication of how receptive the publisher would be to a full proposal. Because a proposal is usually sent out to referee, only submit the full proposal to one publisher at a time. If two or more publishers are interested in receiving the full proposal, order them in preference based on your impressions gathered from corresponding with the commissioning editors and the criteria above.

There are four types of press that publish academic work, each of which tends to specialize in particular kinds of books and have different strategies with regard to production, sales and marketing.

○ **Large, commercial academic presses**

Large, commercial academic presses tend to specialize in publishing textbooks, and to a lesser extent monographs and edited collections. With regard to monographs, they tend to publish texts that they think will have wide appeal or are by writers with established reputations and audience. This is the same for edited collections. Often monographs and edited collections are channelled through book series. The benefits of a commercial academic press are that they tend to have high production values and international distribution and marketing. They are also more likely to offer an advance against royalties to help cover some of the costs of writing the book.

○ Niche commercial presses

Niche publishers focus on specialized texts that might have high appeal to a limited audience. They usually produce a shorter print run, but charge higher retail costs to generate a marginal profit. As a result, they are much more likely to take a chance publishing a text with a limited market, but will not commission a book if it has no commercial viability (remember they too need to be profitable to be sustainable). Some niche presses also support 'vanity publishing', wherein the author pays in full or part for their book to be published.

○ University presses

The university presses have a different brief from commercial publishers. They tend to concentrate on high-quality monographs and edited collections with intrinsic academic worth (rather than commercial potential). Many are run as not-for-profit ventures, sometimes having some of their costs covered by sponsors, donors or endowments. That said, they still need to cover their staffing, production and post-production costs and it is unlikely that they will commission a book that will not cover its costs in sales. Presses vary in their size, the number of titles they publish each year, and the areas of interest they specialize in. Proposals, and in many cases final manuscripts, are likely to be refereed by internal and external reviewers and subject to a faculty selection committee before commissioning or publication. The benefits of publishing with a university press are their generally good reputation for quality (the university after all has staked its name against the manuscript) and that they are likely to be more sympathetic to material that has limited market appeal.

○ Trade presses

Trade presses are aimed at a general, lay readership. As a result they are not interested in academic work unless it is written specifically for a non-academic audience (for example, popular science or biography). The benefit of trade presses is that they are more likely to aggressively market your book to a wide audience beyond academia.

Publishing your PhD

In some countries (such as Finland) it is an accepted practice that PhDs are published. In these cases, the university is usually the publisher. However, in the Anglophone world commercial presses (including university presses) are not generally interested in publishing a PhD thesis. As a rule, theses are too narrowly focused and written for a very select audience, both of which limits their commercial potential. After all, the thesis was written for a specific purpose – to demonstrate expertise and original research with respect to a defined topic – not as a commercial product.

In general, a thesis is written at a stage in a researcher's career when they are learning to write well. Nearly all theses undergo significant revisions whilst being drafted under the guidance of a supervisor or panel. The finished product is often staid, formulaic, exhaustive, repetitive and dull, although it serves its purpose (Luey, 2002). It is perhaps no surprise to find that many academics pick up their thesis after a few years think it amateurish and embarrassing; they have progressed as a writer and academic. Despite this, some university presses might be interested if the thesis is exceptional and makes a significant contribution to a field. Even then, however, the text will probably require substantial revision to make it commercially viable.

Given the difficulty of getting a PhD published as a book, and the emphasis on refereed journal articles for academic accounting and career progression, it may make more sense to publish various bits of a thesis as a set of articles (though see Chapter 5 regarding 'salami publishing'). At a later date, these articles, along with subsequent research, could be drawn together to form the basis of a book with wider appeal.

REFERENCES
Luey, B. (2002) *Handbook for Academic Authors*, 4th edn. Cambridge: Cambridge University Press.

Turner, B. (2004) *The Writers' Handbook*. London: Pan Books.

11 WRITING AND SUBMITTING A BOOK PROPOSAL

A book proposal is designed to convince a commissioning editor, and any experts employed, as to the academic and commercial value of the proposed text. Effectively the book proposal is a sales pitch. If your pitch fails to impress then the editor will reject the proposal. It is important, then, to make a good first impression. On the one hand, this means submitting a well-written, well-constructed and well-presented proposal. This demonstrates that you can write well, that you can convey a message and that you care about your content. On the other hand, it means detailing concisely what the book will be about and why the publisher should be interested in publishing it. The latter is achieved by providing sufficient detail that the proposal can be appraised with regard to content, list suitability, author assessment and market potential.

● Writing the proposal

The proposal will need to consist of several parts. Publishers often provide guidelines as to what a proposal should contain and these are usually published on their websites. You should follow these guidelines and provide all the information requested. In general, all publishers expect for the following details in the proposal.

○ Preliminaries

At the start of the proposal should be the proposed book title (and subtitle if there is one), along with your name and institutional affiliation. Choosing a title is an important process. Preferably you want a title that gives a clear idea about the book's foci, and is catchy and attractive. Many books try to combine these qualities through the use of a title and sub-title, where the main title aims to grab the browser's attention and the sub-title details specifically the book's foci.

◯ Rationale

This section is a short (200–400 word) summary of the book's aims and scope. It should set out clearly what the book will be about, its principal arguments, and specify why the publisher should want to publish the book (for example, it will fill a significant gap in the market, or it will significantly advance the field). You should state whether your book will be a research monograph, supplementary reading, a core textbook, or a book for general readers.

◯ Contents

Here, you expand the brief synopsis to provide a more detailed outline of the book's contents, detailing the anticipated structure of the book and summarizing the content of each chapter into a short paragraph. If the book is an edited collection, you should state who will be writing each chapter, giving their institutional affiliation and a short biography.

◯ Format and style

This section details the envisaged format of the book: whether there will be any plates, diagrams and tables and, if so, how many; whether there will be unusual features such as colour plates or fold-outs; and whether the book needs to be a certain size (pocketsize, for example). You will also need to state the anticipated 'level' of the text: will it be written for a non-specialist audience, an undergraduate audience (if so, for what year), a postgraduate audience, or for experts. Finally, you need to estimate approximately the length of the finished manuscript. Most publishers anticipate texts between 75,000 and 100,000 words unless there are exceptional circumstances.

◯ Readership and market

Here, you need to detail who you believe the intended reader is, and the extent of the book's market. You should be careful to think about whether the book will be useful to readers in other disciplines and to what extent the book might appeal to an international audience. If the book is intended as a course companion you should detail the types of courses the book might be used on as both a core and supplementary text (it might be useful to provide specific examples).

However, while you want to try to sell your book to the publisher, you should be careful not to overstate your case. Commissioning editors have a good idea as to the likely audience of a proposed book. As one of our own previous commissioning editors puts it:

> If the author has written a very clever book on the connection between cyborg culture, Lefebvrean space and the spatiality of coffee consumption they should look at their own proposal honestly and not suggest that the book would be ideal for first year undergraduate students!

○ Competition

This section should provide details of other books about the same topic, highlighting how your book will differ in material, emphasis, style and quality, and why it will be a preferred buy in comparison to already existing books.

○ Timetable

Here you should state a *realistic* delivery date of the completed manuscript. You should be careful to give yourself enough time to complete the task. A useful addition is some indication of when particular milestones might be met, such as an anticipated completion of certain chapters, initial full draft, and final draft.

○ About the author

This section should provide a *brief* synopsis of your career and detail your key publications (including any previous books or editorial experience). It should not be your complete curriculum vitae – if the publisher is interested they will ask for this document separately.

○ Length

In general a book proposal should be no more than eight to ten pages. It should be long enough to sell the idea but short enough to be read and digested quickly. An overly long or badly written/structured proposal will look unprofessional and will lead to rejection (if the author cannot write a decent proposal, how can it be expected that they can undertake the much more demanding task of writing a good book?).

It is important to remember that the proposal will need to be tailored for the type of publisher you envisage publishing your text.

Submitting the proposal

Once a proposal has been drafted and a suitable publisher chosen, the proposal should be submitted to the relevant commissioning editor. A commissioning editor is the contact point between author and publisher; their role is to liaise with authors, evaluate proposals and manuscripts, put books into production, and manage a list of titles published by a publisher. For authors, the commissioning editor is a key gatekeeper. They must be convinced by your book proposal and become its champion within the publishing company.

The submission should include the full proposal and a brief covering letter. The letter should state that you would like the editor to consider the book proposal with respect to commissioning the full book for publication by the press the editor represents. It might also state why that particular press is being approached and how the book might fit into their wider portfolio of publications. It is standard practice to send the proposal to one publisher at a time.

As detailed by Clark (1994: 69–70), the commissioning editor needs to be convinced of the worthiness of your project in respect of a number of factors:

○ Suitability for list

The editor will assess whether the proposed book fits with the other titles in the publisher's catalogue. Publishers tend to specialize and build a reputation around a few topics aimed at particular target audiences. The 'fit' will thus depend on style, content, the direction the editor wishes the list to take, and so on. For example, if the publisher specializes in textbooks, it is unlikely to publish a monograph; if it specializes in natural sciences it is unlikely to be interested in a book on comparative religion. As noted above, before submitting a proposal you need to undertake basic background research into different publishers and approach one whose list you think your book would complement.

○ Author assessment

By commissioning a book, the editor is effectively investing in the author. They will therefore make a judgement on the author's ability to deliver a marketable manuscript. To do this they will evaluate the author's qualifications, public standing, motivations, drive and so on. This does not mean that they will only invest in established talent. Commissioning editors are always on the lookout for talented first-time authors, hoping that they will sign them up before their rivals and develop a long-term working relationship with them.

○ Content

If the editor feels the topic fits within their list and feels that the author is capable of delivering a good manuscript, they will then assess the potential content of the book in terms of breadth and depth of coverage, structure and suitability for the intended audience. If they are unsure, they might ask to see a sample chapter and, as detailed below, they often seek advice from experts within the relevant field whose opinion they trust.

○ Market

Again, it should never be forgotten that the publishing industry is precisely that, an industry. For publishers to stay in business they need to sell books. While there is a degree of altruism amongst commissioning editors, it is becoming increasingly rare, as each book they commission and publish is expected to turn a profit. Not only does the editor's job depend on it, but also the future of the company. Therefore, the bottom line for nearly all editors is whether a book will sell sufficient copies to cover all its costs and return a profit. No matter how interesting the topic, if you cannot convince the publisher of that, they will not commission it.

○ Competition

As noted, it is extremely rare that a book is the first published on a topic. The editor will therefore compare your proposed book with existing books to determine the advantages of your text *vis-à-vis* existing texts and whether there is a gap in the market.

Using these criteria, the commissioning editor will read your proposal carefully and make an initial judgement based upon their own experience and knowledge of the types of book their company publishes. If they feel your proposal is weak or more suited to another publisher they will inform you of their decision, providing a summary of their reasons. While their decision might be disappointing, you should reflect on any advice they give and use it to strengthen your proposal.

If they are interested in the proposal they will usually send it out to a panel of two or three experts (and sometimes more depending on the proposal) to ask their opinion as to the merits of the book envisaged and to confirm their own assessment. The panel is usually asked to comment on the following to give an overall recommendation with regard to commissioning:

- The originality and value of the proposed text
- The appropriateness of the content and how it is structured
- The quality of the proposal *vis-à-vis* other texts
- Whether the author's assessment of the market is realistic
- How the proposed text might be strengthened
- The author's standing within a field and whether the author is capable of editing/writing the text

This process usually takes a couple of months, but may take longer if the publisher has difficulty finding suitable reviewers willing to undertake the task. The reviews and the commissioning editor's decision will be sent to you. If the panel's assessment is negative, then the commissioning editor will usually follow their advice unless the editor feels very strongly (based on their instinct and experience) that the book will sell well. Sometimes, the author is requested to revise the proposal on the advice of the reviewers. If you have not heard from the publisher within three months of the proposal being sent out for review, contact them and ask for an update and a date by which you might hear the decision. Do not contact them again for another update until after this date.

Once the reviewers comments are back, if they are positive and the editor wants to commission the book they will often produce a production cost sheet (sometimes this is done before sending the proposal to referees). This uses the information in the proposal (such as length, format, number of illustrations) plus the editor's experience of market and likely cost price of the published book to create a spreadsheet of anticipated costs and potential profit. On the basis of the reports and the spreadsheet the editor will take the proposal to an editorial committee and make a case for offering a contract. This committee usually consists of a senior editor, subject editors, marketing and sales managers. On the basis of the evidence presented to them they will either approve or reject the proposal. Sometimes they might approve the proposal subject to revisions in foci, content or style.

If the referee's comments are negative, but the publisher is still interested in the proposal, they might send the comments back to you and ask for a response. In effect, the editor is providing an opportunity to strengthen the proposal and to explain why the referees might have got it wrong. If a convincing case is made, the editor will then take the proposal to the editorial committee for approval.

For an introduction to the book publishing industry from a commissioning editor's point of view, see Clark (1994) and Davies (1995).

What if a publisher has approached you to write a book?

Commissioning editors, through talking to their existing authors and delegates at conferences, and monitoring the sales of their lists, usually have a pretty good idea as to what topics are 'hot' or where there are gaps in the market. If no prospective authors approach them to write a book on these identified topics they will adopt a proactive role and approach potential authors directly. While it can be very flattering to be asked to write or edit a text, you should think carefully through the proposition before coming to a decision. As noted, writing or editing a book is a major undertaking and should not be entered into lightly. There are four key issues that you need to weigh up.

The first consideration is *motivation*, and is the most important. Do you really want to write or edit a book on the proposed topic? Is it a project that excites you, that you would relish doing? If you are not enthusiastic about the proposed text at the outset, then our advice is not to proceed with the project – it will simply act as a millstone around your neck, diverting your energies from projects you really want to undertake. There might, of course, be other factors that influence your decision, related for example to career progression. In these cases, you need to evaluate the potential benefits of authoring or editing a text against your enthusiasm for the project.

Assuming you have the motivation to undertake the project, the second consideration is *time*. Most people engaged in active research are very busy and are often over-committed. If this is the case, then you need to ask yourself how you are going to fit this new project into an already full schedule of existing commitments. It might mean simply taking on a larger burden or dropping other projects to make space. There might also be the possibility to negotiate with the commissioning editor, suggesting that you are prepared to undertake the task but that you want any proposed timetable extended, so that you start the writing or editing at some point in the future, say a year's time, when some other projects have been completed, thereby freeing up some time.

The third consideration is the degree of *freedom to shape the content* of the proposed book. Given that it is the commissioning editor who has conceived the need for a text, they may well have their own vision for the scope, content and format. This vision may well be different from the type of book you envisage writing. Before entering into any agreement to author or edit a text it is essential that both your visions come into line around a common understanding of the proposed text. This will normally necessitate some negotiation. If it is clear that your vision of the text is substantially different from the editor's then do not agree to write the book; it will only lead to problems at a later date. If your appetite has been whetted, however, and you now want to pursue writing a text on your vision of this topic, then write a proposal and submit it to another publisher.

The fourth consideration is *resourcing and reward*. Most academic authors are not looking to make a lot of money from publishing; they are more interested in communicating their ideas and developing their careers. At the same time, most do not want to be out of pocket for their efforts, and will want to recoup any costs incurred. Therefore, if the project requires certain expenses, it is useful to know whether the publisher is willing to cover the costs. Also, are the proposed royalty rates acceptable? In other words, is the project worth undertaking besides the obvious benefits of publishing a book?

Having thought through these issues and assuming that you want to undertake the proposed topic, then the commissioning editor will ask you to write a book proposal and to proceed through the usual commissioning process.

 ## What if you have already written the book?

Most researchers seek a publishing contract before drafting the book; that way they are more certain that their efforts will not be in vain. There is a number of reasons, however, as to why you might write the book in advance of seeking a publisher. It may be the case that you might not have a clear idea of the finished product ahead of starting and you want to see how the book develops before approaching a publisher. By drafting the book without a publisher, you can be certain that you will end up with the book that you wanted to write, rather than the book the publisher wanted. Without a contract, there are no pressures from the publisher, particularly related to timing. Of course, it may simply be that you did not manage to secure a contract, but that you were determined to write the text. Whatever the case, once the text is completed, the hunt for a publisher begins.

In terms of selecting a publisher to approach, we suggest that you follow the advice presented in Chapter 10. Once you have chosen a publisher, our advice is to send the appropriate commissioning editor a synopsis of the book, outlining its rationale and its potential market, along with two or three sample chapters and a brief biography. If the publisher is interested they will ask for the entire manuscript to evaluate. If you have difficulty securing publication, rather than simply continuing to send the manuscript to potential publishers it may be more constructive to reflect on any reasons they give for rejection and to act on any advice. If you are determined to try to publish the manuscript as completed, however, then perseverance may be the key. There are literally thousands of publishers, all catering to different authors and markets. Another alternative might be vanity publishing (see Chapter 10) or self-publication (see Chapter 15).

REFERENCES

Clark, G. (1994) *Inside Book Publishing*, 2nd edn. London: Routledge.

Davies, G. (1995) *Book Commissioning and Acquisition*. London: Routledge.

12 NEGOTIATING A BOOK CONTRACT

Once an editorial board within the publishing company has approved the proposal for commissioning, the publisher will issue you with a standard contract.

Any contract issued by a publisher should be read very carefully so that you are aware of the exact terms and conditions to which you are agreeing. *Never* sign a contract until you have read it and you are confident you understand what you are committing to. All authors or editors have to sign the contract, not just the lead author. The contract then not only binds you to the publisher, but also to your colleagues. You may have an agreement with colleagues as to who will do what in producing the manuscript. The publisher is unlikely to recognize this division of labour and if your colleagues let you down, you will have to complete their work to fulfil the contract (publishers are interested in a complete product not bits of it).

While experienced (and successful) authors often have latitude to negotiate the terms of their contract it is fair to say that this will be more difficult for first-time authors. That said, if there is any clause you are unhappy with or want to query you should contact the commissioning editor. If after negotiation you remain dissatisfied with the contract you are under no obligation to sign. One option here might be to withdraw the proposal and approach another publisher. If you do this though, it is unlikely that the first publisher will entertain publishing the book if you are unsuccessful finding a new publisher.

The contract usually consists of several parts detailing both the publisher's and your obligations and the penalties for non-compliance. These include:

- *Grants*: the rights the contract grants to the publisher
- *Publisher's warranty*: what the publisher agrees to comply with
- *Author's warranty*: what the author agrees to comply with
- *Copyright*: who retains copyright of the published work
- *Moral rights*: your right to be identified as the author of the text

- *Permissions*: who pays for permission to reproduce copyrighted material
- *Delivery and condition of the manuscript*: the terms under which you will deliver the manuscript
- *Royalties*: the percentage of the net sale price you will receive for each book sold (see below for a fuller discussion)
- *Subsidiary rights*: what you will receive if the book is translated or reproduced in another format
- *Statements and payments*: when the publisher will provide you with statements and royalty payments
- *Tax*: how the publisher will deal with the tax relating to monies earned by the author
- *Author's copies*: how many free copies of the book you are entitled to, plus any author discount on purchasing further copies
- *New editions*: the obligations of authors and publishers with regard to updating and revising the text
- *Option*: a clause that means that you will have to give first refusal of your next book to the publisher
- *Termination*: the terms under which the contract can be terminated
- *Infringement action*: what the publisher will do if a third party infringes your rights as an author
- *Notices*: the means by which official communication between publisher and author must be undertaken
- *Arbitration*: the process by which a disagreement between author and publisher will be arbitrated
- *Legal jurisdiction*: the jurisdiction under which the contract is valid and can be contested.

Royalties

In terms of royalties, rates vary slightly between publishers but are generally between 7.5 and 12 per cent of the net income for an authored text (depending on factors such as whether the book is a monograph or textbook, the author's track record, and so on) and between 3 and 7.5 per cent for an edited collection. The rate might rise after a certain number of copies have been sold. Sometimes there is a difference in the rate between paperback and hardback editions.

You should note that royalties are most often calculated on net receipts rather than sale price. So 10 per cent net receipts means 10 per cent *after* the bookseller has taken their slice (about 35–40 per cent in the UK and 38–45 per cent outside). As Luey (2002) notes, this is often a source of confusion and agitation for authors. They know the book is priced at say $30, they receive 10 per cent royalties and 1000 copies of the book were printed; as a result they often expect to earn $3000 (which for many first-time authors seems a very low amount for the effort expended in any case). However, the slice for the bookseller needs to be removed, many copies are often given away to reviewers and as gratis copies to academics who might adopt the book as a course text, and of course not all of the 1000 printed are necessarily sold (or are offered at a discount price to help sales). All of this means that an author often receives less than they anticipated. The assumption is that the publisher is doing very well at the expense of the author. In actual fact, this is most often not the case. The publisher has to cover the costs of its editing and production staff, and its typesetting, printing, binding, marketing and distribution costs. If a book sells the full print run, the publisher will make a marginal profit. If the book sells poorly it will make a loss. Of course, if the book sells very well and demands a reprint the publisher makes a larger profit, but then so does the author.

You should also note that even if a contract for a hardback book specifies paperback royalties, this does not necessarily mean a paperback will be produced. You should ask the editor directly if a paperback version will be published.

Most academic books sell relatively few copies. We have heard more than one commissioning editor state that an academic book (excluding textbooks) that sells more than 1000 copies in a year is a bestseller (with many selling far less). Many authors get disheartened by such sales and blame publishers for not adequately marketing their text. While warranted in some cases, it is simply a fact of publishing that academic texts have small audiences (delimited by the number of researchers within a specialist field, who of course do not buy every text published on their research focus). This is not to say that these texts have no worth; they are read and valued by a select audience of peers and they can be a significant factor in career development.

The exception to low sales and income is textbooks. A well-written textbook that is widely adopted will generate significant incomes for both author and publisher. As a result the textbook sector is highly competitive. A consequence of the competition is that many textbooks fail to generate large sales because they do not become a standard text and thus only have a small market share. Textbooks, then, are not a guaranteed source of high income, but have the most potential to be so.

What this all means is that very few academic authors make a lot of money directly from publishing; and hardly any generate enough income that they could make a decent living from it. This is not to say that they do not benefit financially from writing a book. In addition to the royalties they receive, authors often benefit from salary increases attached to promotion, in part gained through their publications. If finance is the motivator for writing a book, it is from this latter source that the money is often made.

 ## Advances

An advance is a sum of money paid to an author in advance of the book being published. It is a token of good faith and is designed to pay for expenses incurred in researching and writing the book. An advance is not a payment in addition to royalties and the sum will be deducted from the first royalty cheque. In some cases, publishers will divide up the advance with so much paid on receipt of a signed contract, so much on receipt of chapter drafts or the final manuscript, and the final instalment on publication. Some publishers will offer an advance as a matter of course, in other cases if you desire an advance payment you will have to ask for one. The amount you receive will be directly related to your past publication record, your relationship to the publisher and the projected sales of the proposed book. Of course, if the book manuscript does not materialize then you may well be expected to pay back any payments you have received.

 ## Subventions

A subvention is a request from the publisher for the author to defray some of the costs of publication. It is different from vanity publishing in that the publisher is not expecting to receive the whole cost of publication and is still enforcing high standards of content. Usually a publisher might seek a subvention if the book is valuable in terms of its message but aimed at a very narrow market that makes it economically unviable, or the costs associated with producing a text (such as including colour plates) push the retail price beyond what readers are perceived to be willing to pay. In effect a subvention allows a commercially unprofitable book to be produced and distributed. A subvention may be in the region of a couple of thousand US dollars (or equivalent) and many universities have publication grant schemes that can be applied to for such monies. If asked for a subvention, negotiate on price, ask for a clause that ensures it will be repaid if the book does sell well, and ask for help from the publisher in finding a third party (small foundations, etc.) to pay the cost (Luey, 2002).

On signing the contract

Remember, in signing a contract you are authorizing a legal document that binds you and your proposed text to that company. In effect you are officially starting a working relationship that will last for years – while the book is written, while it is in production, and while it is still in print and being sold. Like all relationships it will need to be worked at and nurtured. While at times the relationship might become strained for all sorts of reasons (often as much a fault of authors/editors as the publishers – late delivery of a manuscript, for example), ultimately the book's success is dependent on both parties fulfilling their obligations. This necessitates understanding and respect for each other, and a willingness to resolve differences of opinion amicably.

Tax

As noted, while publishing a book is an enormously rewarding experience, it can also be financially rewarding. Book income is an additional source of finance, that is, it is in addition to any salary and as such will need to be declared to the tax authorities, even if it consists of very small payments. Of course, in writing the book it is likely that you incurred some expenditure. In general these expenses can be offset against any tax due. Our advice is to employ a financial consultant or an accountant to advise you of your obligations and how to proceed. Failing to declare book income, even if it is earned in another jurisdiction, is an offence and is likely to lead to problems with tax inspectors.

REFERENCES
Luey, B. (2002) *Handbook for Academic Authors*, 4th edn. Cambridge: Cambridge University Press.

13 WRITING A BOOK

Once the contract has been signed the book actually needs to be written! This task can be quite daunting, even for an established author. A book provides a larger stage on which to express ideas and disseminate research than any other form of publication. But like a large theatrical production, it is a demanding task to fill it evenly and consistently throughout with interest and quality, while also retaining composition and narrative structure. The book needs to communicate clearly and effectively, while being balanced, well-conceived and structured. Books, then, tend to be crafted and are less formulaic than many articles in style and structure. The 'story' the book tells needs to be carefully blended together so that it draws the reader through a much longer and complex narrative than an article or conference presentation. Marshalling and organizing large amounts of information, evidence, ideas and argument into an effective narrative takes skill, time and patience; three things that are often over- or under-estimated by prospective authors.

 ## Project management

All of the general writing advice contained in Chapter 4 holds for writing a book. What distinguishes a book from other forms of writing is the size of the task. Writing a book is a major undertaking and should be treated as a major project in itself, rather than simply the end product of a larger research project. As such, it needs to be carefully plotted and managed to ensure that the venture stays on track. Marrying the book proposal to a projected timeline is a useful exercise, detailing particular milestones to be met at certain dates. If on-going research is needed then this needs to be planned in advance to tie in to the writing schedule. Once a work timetable has been set it is important to try to stick to it as it may prove difficult to catch up at a later date. If the book is a collaborative venture you should be careful to ensure that all parties know their role, the tasks they have to undertake and when these tasks have to be completed. It is vital that there is good communication between collaborators and that each party is kept informed of progress. A good strategy is to ensure that each phase of the writing project has a coordinator who is responsible for its management.

What do you do if you know you are not going to keep to time?

Many writers under-estimate the time it takes to complete a manuscript. Or rather, they estimate the correct amount of time if ideal conditions prevail, but do not allow for the occurrence of other events or projects. Most researchers are under pressure to take on commitments such as new research projects, writing journal articles, teaching extra courses, extra administrative tasks and so on. These all place pressures on time allocated to drafting a manuscript. If it becomes clear that the manuscript is not going to be completed on schedule you should inform your commissioning editor, outlining the reasons why, and providing a new timetable until completion. Failing to inform your commissioning editor and hoping the problems go away will not serve either you or your publisher well. In regard to the former, you need to maintain a cordial working relationship; after all, you are reliant on the publisher to print and sell your book. In regard to the latter, the publisher needs to be able to plan their catalogues, production and marketing. As the date for anticipated delivery of your manuscript approaches the publisher will start to activate their procedures for receiving and processing it. If they know that the manuscript will be late, they can re-jig their plans and schedules.

Keeping focus

Given the size and scope of a book project it is easy to lose sight of the overall ambition of the text, and for the narrative to lose coherence, conciseness and focus. It is important to try to stick to the original plan, and to concentrate on the designated topic and argument. In other words, you should be careful not to use the opportunity of a large canvas to drift into elaborating issues tangential to the focus. The publisher might have provided a large canvas, but they expect a detailed, balanced and sharp image, not an abstract, disconnected, poorly structured one. They will also expect a manuscript that fulfils what was a commissioned. So, if the contract was for a textbook then they will expect a text that is suitable for students. If you provide a research monograph that purports to be 'student-friendly' they are likely to demand a significant re-write.

Indeed, it is important to keep in mind that a contract only binds the publisher to print and distribute a book *if* they are satisfied that it fulfils the aims and objectives of the proposal (that is to say the book submitted is the one proposed), that it is the right length and contains the agreed number of tables, figures, etc. (so that their production costs remain the same), and that the quality of the manuscript meets expectation. In other words, the author has honoured their part of the contract.

This is not to say that the book has to stick faithfully to the plan outlined in the proposal. Publishers accept that the content of a book often tends to mutate during the writing phase as authors develop their ideas through reading, researching and drafting a text. Certainly this book evolved during its drafting, changing its title (several times), its chapter structure and the number of chapters, and so on. It did, however, stay faithful to its brief of providing a handbook that explains the processes of publication and how to successfully communicate research to the wider world. That is to say, that while the book mutated, we did fulfil our part of the contract.

A strong commissioning editor *will* demand that original focus is kept, and *will* require you to tighten up a manuscript, to remove extraneous text and to produce a text that is more readable and marketable, if they feel that you have deviated from what was commissioned and they are not happy with the result. The easiest way to avoid major revisions is to keep the writing project tightly focused and to resist extending, expanding or deviating from the original brief. If for some reason, such as there being a significant new development in the field, you feel that the focus needs to change or some additional chapters should be added you should consult with your commissioning editor before progressing to make sure they are happy with the proposed changes.

 ## Creating a text that 'works'

As noted, given the size of a book manuscript, creating a text that 'works' is more of a challenge than writing an article or report. By 'works' we mean the text tells a 'story' in an effective and engaging way. For a text to work well the narrative has to work across chapters and within chapters; the argument and evidence are logically structured across the whole manuscript, leading the reader through the 'story'. Generally there should be a balance between evidence with reasoned argument, and the ideas of others and of the author. The length of each chapter should also be kept reasonably consistent.

Getting the structure right can be quite difficult, especially when the text has to introduce a wide variety of complex concepts and evidence that need to be compared and contrasted. A highly skilled writer is one who can organize such complexity in a way that makes the debates clear to the reader. To create such lucidity might mean playing around with the text, restructuring the chapters or content within a chapter, or moving content between chapters. As a consequence, it is not unusual for a manuscript to go through several drafts as all the material is fitted together in different ways in order to find the version that works best. A useful strategy in this process is to ask friends or colleagues to assess a draft of the manuscript. They can provide valuable guidance as to whether the narrative is well structured and engaging, and provide suggestions as to alterations. Their advice is usually best heeded as less sympathetic reviewers of the published manuscript will almost certainly pick-up and critique the same points.

 ## Sections unique to books

While books have most of the same requirements as other forms of printed media in terms of structure and narrative, they can also have some sections or structural arrangements that are unique to the book form, although none of these is essential.

Dedication
It is quite common for books to include a dedication page. They are usually quite simple, stating the name or names of those to whom the book is dedicated.

Preliminaries
The preliminaries ('prelims') detail a book's content and include a table of all contents plus listings of tables and plates where appropriate. The table of

contents usually lists the chapters by number, title and the page number at which the chapter starts. In some cases it will also include major sub headings, again with page numbers. The listings of tables and plates detail the table or plate number, the title (often known as the legend of caption) and page number.

Preface

The preface provides a short introduction to the book (rather than simply to the subject matter). It usually explains the motivation for, and background to, writing the text, and its scope and purpose.

Foreword

A foreword is a short introduction to the book written by someone other than the author(s) or editor(s) and is usually by a person familiar with the book's target audience. Primarily, a foreword is an endorsement of the book's content.

Parts

Some books, particularly those that are quite lengthy or multifaceted, are divided not only into chapters, but also into numbered parts that group chapters together. In some cases a part will have a short introduction or précis to the following chapters. A part will usually have a title indicating the theme linking that group of chapters.

Notes

Notes that accompany a text are usually grouped at the end of the chapter they appear in, or at the end of manuscript. The notes provide additional material that supplements or illustrates an argument but was not deemed suitable to include in the text itself, or provide links to relevant literature.

Glossary

A glossary is usually provided at the end of a text that contains technical terms that are likely to be unfamiliar to an audience. It is an alphabetical listing of these terms with a short explanatory description.

Appendices

Appendices usually consist of supplementary materials that are useful to an argument but are too detailed or lengthy to be included in the text itself. They might consist of technical details, transcripts or other forms of data, various analyses, case study material and sections of other published reports or documents. In the latter case, permission to produce such material must be sought (see Chapter 5).

Index

The index provides a means to search the book for passages about certain topics. It consists of a listing of keywords accompanied by the page numbers where these items are discussed. Keywords can consist of scientific terms, topics or people's names. The index is not completed until the final proofs have been produced to ensure page number accuracy (see Chapter 18).

 # Submitting the manuscript

Depending on what has been agreed with the commissioning editor, the manuscript may be submitted in one of two ways. Either sample chapters will be delivered as they are written, or the entire manuscript will be submitted as a completed script. The commissioning editor, and possibly one or two chosen experts, will check the script on delivery for length, style, completeness and quality. Generally, publishers will want two complete copies of the script, plus a version on a floppy disk or CD. The script should be presented:

- Double-spaced
- In a 12 point type size and a clear, readable font
- Printed on only one side of the paper
- With page numbers throughout.

In some cases the commissioning editor might ask you for one or two recommendations with regard to reviewers. Select reviewers whom you know to be well-respected names in your field and who seem fair and broadminded; ideally they will be people you know from conferences and so on, but not people that the editor will know to be close colleagues or friends (after all the editor wants a relatively objective view of the work). Depending on their opinion of the selected reviewers, the editor will either choose your nominees or select alternatives.

If either the commissioning editor or the reviewers are unhappy with any aspect of the text then you will be asked to revise the script. If you feel particularly strongly that the changes requested would detract from your script, you are entitled to challenge them. If the publisher is insisting that they be undertaken you have two options: either comply, or cancel the contract and seek another publisher (although this course of action is not without implications – see Chapter 12). Generally some kind of compromise can be agreed. Once the text has been accepted for publication it will enter production (see Chapter 18).

14 EDITING A BOOK OR SPECIAL ISSUE

Edited collections normally arise from one of two main sources. The first source is a conference (or conference session). Here, potential contributors will have been (largely) pre-identified and organized to talk about a particular theme or set of themes. After the event the potential editor(s) select the best contributions for the edited collection. In addition, they may approach potential authors from outside of that collection. In some cases a commissioning editor might be approached prior to the event to gauge the potential interest of a publisher and encourage potential participants to attend.

The second main source for the development of edited collections (both research and teaching-oriented) is through the vision of one or more (co-) editors who draw together a set of authors prepared to write on a defined topic. These editors approach a commissioning editor directly with a view to securing a publishing contract. In this case, contributions are commissioned, and the content of the chapters is often more tightly defined by the editors than is the case for papers arising from conferences. Whatever the source of the collection, it is probably the relationship between editor(s) and these (potential) contributors that has the biggest impact on the 'quality' of the final product.

 ## Excellent communication

It is essential that you develop and maintain excellent communications with your contributing authors from the outset of any edited project for two reasons. First, edited texts can sometimes be tricky projects to manage *per se*, simply because of the number of people that can be involved. Secondly, while it is probably agreed that the 'best' edited texts are those that are produced through what is commonly referred to as 'strong' editorship, such strength does not necessarily mean working with a complete disregard for the contributor's other responsibilities, stress levels and/or sanity – the relationship between editor(s) and contributor need not be one of 'master and servant'. Instead, you should endeavour to be clear in your expectations – you need to explain how you envisage the relationship working at the outset of any commission, explaining fully your vision for the overall book and any specific requirements or areas of focus for the individual authors. If this is achieved, and agreed early on, you are more likely to receive the chapter you commissioned, rather than the chapter the author might have written if given total free rein.

 ## Clear expectations

Contributors require a clear understanding of a number of key elements that delimit an edited collection. One such element concerns the rationale for the collection – why it is being produced and why it will represent an important contribution to the body of knowledge. This will help prospective authors to situate their ideas/chapter in a broader academic context. This can be followed by an outline of the aims of the collection, providing the authors with a tighter indication of the scope of their individual chapters. All authors should also be provided with details of the proposed contents of the book, enabling them to place their contributions in relation to the other chapters. One way to aid continuity is for the editors to provide each author with an initial draft of the collection's introduction well in advance of when the individual chapters are requested for submission.

In sum, 'strong editorship' would perhaps suggest that the clearer and more succinct the focus specified, the better. This might be achieved by detailing one or two key questions or issues that the participants should address or build their contributions around. That said, however, there is clearly a balance to be struck between gaining a collection of interesting, engaging and varied contributions focused around the key issue(s) in question/focus, and exerting too prescriptive an influence which might ultimately disenchant what could still be prospective authors, most of whom are likely to appreciate, if not expect, some degree of academic freedom/licence.

Finally, and moving away from issues of content, the authors should also be provided with specific details concerning the format and word length of their chapter, and the envisaged framework/timescale for the collection's production. Much of this may depend on discussions (previous, or yet to be held) between the collection editor(s) and the commissioning editor of the volume.

Keeping on track

Occasional gentle prodding of authors at particular times as they draft their chapters or papers will make it more likely that the text will be completed on time. As a general rule, enquire as to progress half way through the writing period, send a reminder a month before the chapter is due and ask whether the deadline will be met, and if the chapter is late send a strong reminder one month after the deadline. If the chapter is still not forthcoming then you will need to liaise with the author to see whether it will ever materialize and, if it will, to agree a new work plan. Be careful not to overly monitor authors, particularly if it is still before an agreed deadline, but do not be afraid to take a hard line if required, especially if the whole project is being held up. It might in some cases be necessary to cut your losses and to drop a chapter/paper that is holding up the publication of the book/special issue. Remember, while overly strong editorship can be stifling and frustrating, overly weak editorship can lead to edited collections with little overall coherence and poor links between chapters/papers.

 # Refereeing and editing an author's text

Once a draft chapter has been submitted the task of the editor is to read and critique it, checking that the content follows the brief given, that the text meets any length requirements, and that it is appropriately structured and styled. As an editor you can either suggest or insist on changes to the text before accepting it for publication. Remember, chapters/papers that are poorly conceived and weakly written will detract from the overall collection. If there is more than one editor make sure that each editor has a defined role (for example, each editor looks after a certain number of authors) and that there is good communication between editors to ensure coordination and avoid duplication.

Alternatively, maintaining coherence across chapters, and providing comments to authors, can be addressed in more imaginative and collective ways that perhaps help unsettle traditional hierarchies between editor and contributor. One idea (that, admittedly, from experience certainly looks easier when described than it proves to be in practice!) is to circulate the draft chapters among the authors involved in the collection, allowing them to comment, critique, review, or just simply gain an insight in each other's contributions. This could occur either through allocated, individual peer review, or by making all the submissions available to everyone involved to access, view and comment. This might add to the potential coherence of the collection by attempting to promote dialogue between authors and their positions.

 ## Editing a special issue of a journal

While editing a special issue of a journal has many of the same elements of editing a book it differs with regard to the peer-reviewed nature of journals and their editorial procedures. All article submissions to a journal are peer-reviewed regardless of whether they form part of a special issue. Journals differ in the extent to which they allow special issue editors to take part in the reviewing process. In some cases, the journal editor will allow the special editor free rein to select referees, to send material to them, and to make decisions based on their comments and communicate this to authors. At the other extreme, the special editor will have no say or involvement in the process; they simply bring the papers together and write an editorial once the papers have been accepted for publication. Other journals fall somewhere in between, for example allowing special editors to suggest referee names (although they might not all be used).

As special editor, your first task is to negotiate with the journal editor as to how the process will work and to communicate this with your contributing authors. Next, it is to fulfil whatever role you have negotiated. If your role involves selecting referees and sending material out then you need to obtain appropriate letterhead material, referee report templates and so on, and a full procedure of how the journal normally operates (which you should follow). It might also be useful to ask for anonymous examples of rejection and acceptance letters from the journal editor to give guidance with respect to your own correspondence. Remember, while you might have put the issue together and the contributors may well be friends, if an article is not up to standard you will have to reject it. It might also be useful to employ one referee who will look at the whole issue to make sure it works as a set. If the journal puts all the papers through the refereeing process, make sure you have an agreed timetable and contact the journal editor if you feel things are slipping. Note, however, that the reviewing pace will move at the speed of the slowest referee.

15 SELF-PUBLISHING A BOOK

The benefits of a publisher handling the production and distribution of your manuscript are that you do not have to deal with, and worry about, typesetting, printing, binding, marketing, distribution, managing finances and so on. In effect, you pass on the burden of production and sales, and the potential financial risks, to the publisher. It may be the case, however, that you wish to self-publish your book, either to retain control of content, to realize all the financial rewards, or because you could not secure a publication contract. It is important to realize that by taking the self-publication route, while you gain more control and more of the rewards, you also assume the burdens and the risk.

By far the cheapest, and probably the easiest and most hassle-free option, is self-publication on the Internet (see Chapter 8). If you are determined to produce a hardcopy version that can be sold in shops there are a number of issues you need to think about. The first of these is financial – can you afford to produce a book? All the costs for a book need to be met upfront, with the hope that sales will pay back these costs and generate a profit later.

The way to proceed is to produce a financial model (also see Table 17.2). To construct this model you will need to calculate what work you will do yourself and what needs to be contracted out. Things that you can realistically do include typesetting, cover design, marketing (contacting booksellers and libraries, producing promotional literature), distribution (posting to booksellers) and managing finances. Printing and binding will almost certainly need to be contracted out.

For inputs into the model, you will need to get costings for all the jobs you want to contract out. To do this, you will need to calculate roughly how long the text will be in pages and how many copies of the book you wish to print. As a general rule we would caution against printing more than 500–1000 copies unless you are very confident that you will sell more. As previously noted, most academic books have low sales and most academic publishers only print this many, unless it is a textbook they are going to market aggressively. A good printer will discuss with you issues such as the quality of the paper and the method of binding and give you a range of quotes. For marketing you need to cost for printing promotional material and postage. For distribution you need to cost for package and postage, and also factor in the slice that the bookseller will take. If you want a professionally designed cover, then you will need to source a quote from a graphic designer. It may well be the case that you will want to investigate setting up a company to front your enterprise.

Once you have produced a financial model that you are happy with, then you need to construct a production schedule. This schedule should list all the tasks that need to be undertaken and by what dates. It is important to implement and enforce this schedule, as you will need to book certain jobs in advance such as the printing. You should be realistic about this schedule – you will not get everything achieved in a week. As a general rule a book takes forty weeks from submission of manuscript to bookshelf if produced by a professional publisher. While it might not take this long, self-publishing will take at least a few weeks. On your schedule should be layout design, typesetting, proofing, indexing, obtaining an ISBN, ensuring copyright, cover design, cover proofing, printing, binding, preliminary marketing, contacting booksellers, setting up of accompanying book website (if desired) and distribution. Each of these tasks will need to be done to professional standards as your intended audience will expect as much.

Your book (whether it be printed, on the Internet, or published in another form such as Braille or CD or audio tape) will need a unique numerical identification code – International Standard Book Number (ISBN) – that allows individuals, publishers, book suppliers and libraries worldwide to locate and order it. To obtain an ISBN you will need to purchase one from the assigned national or regional agency in the country the book is being published. For details on ISBN agencies see http://www.isbn-international.org/agencies.html. This website also gives full details of ISBN use and policy. It is possible to get a barcode issued to accompany the ISBN and details of the book, and a number of Internet companies offer this service.

Like all published and unpublished documents, your work will be protected by copyright law, a form of intellectual property law. Typically, a notice of copyright is printed in the preliminary pages using a copyright symbol ©, or the word 'Copyright', followed by the year of first publication and the name of the copyright owner, in this case your own name. For example, the copyright for this book is stated on the reverse of the title page as © Rob Kitchin and Duncan Fuller 2005. Although not required, you can register your work for copyright protection and thus create a legal statement for public record of your ownership. Registering the copyright provides a sound legal basis for challenging any infringement by a third party, which without registration might be difficult to prove. To register copyright you will need to contact the agency responsible for copyright laws in your jurisdiction, in the US, the US Copyright Office (http://www.copyright.gov/register/), and in the UK, the UK Copyright Service (http://www.copyrightservice.co.uk/copyright/registering(04).htm). In both cases there is a small fee to be paid.

With regard to marketing and distribution, it is important to note that it may be difficult to get booksellers and libraries to stock and sell a self-published book, as they prefer to deal with established publishers. It might be especially difficult with regard to booksellers and libraries from beyond your region/country. Support can be gained by registering your ISBN with a company such as R.R. Bowker (http://www.bowkerlink.com), who will provide free listings in various directories used by booksellers.

Perhaps the best way to market and sell the book is using the Internet. Online booksellers such as Amazon will give you international sales and distribution. Alternatively, you might prefer setting up a website that details the book and allows interested readers to purchase online, though you may have to contract expert help to set up secure credit card purchasing in order to accept and process online orders. Selling this way will increase the revenue by removing the sum payable to the bookseller. A further, key avenue for sales is through word of mouth. Here, reviews in relevant journals/newsletters might play an important role. Sending details of the book, plus order details, to relevant mailing lists might also be an option. Finally, a book launch could be organized; inviting those whom you think might be interested in the book, plus representatives of any relevant media. For those serious about self-publishing there are a number of guides to consult (see Appendix 1).

16 PROPOSING A NEW JOURNAL OR BOOK SERIES

As well as publishing individual books, publishers also produce periodicals and consolidate books into series of related texts. Both ventures can be extremely profitable – through generating long-term subscriptions and libraries/individuals buying a series of books rather than single volumes – and publishers are usually keen to explore new journal or book series ideas. Generally they will be looking for novel ideas that fill a niche or tackle an existing subject from a new perspective. When thinking about proposing a new journal or book series you should be mindful of two things: generally publishers will want editors who have editorial experience and extensive networks; and as detailed in Chapters 14 and 17, editing a journal or book series is a lot of work, especially in the case of a journal where a new edition has to be produced regularly.

Proposing a new academic journal

Starting a new academic journal requires a major commitment from a publisher. It means a long-term commitment to produce, market and distribute a highly specific product aimed at a very particular target audience. Start-up costs are high, with cost recovery slow. In established disciplines, where there are already a number of journals, a publisher might not expect to break even on their initial investment for several years as individuals and libraries evaluate the journal and decide whether to invest in it long term. Given the current economic climate and the cutbacks in library budgets, libraries are often cautious about subscribing to a new journal. In new fields and disciplines, publishers might expect a more rapid take-up, but also have to contend and compete with other start-up journals seeking to fill the niche. On the other hand, if the journal is successful then the publisher has a long-term, guaranteed source of income and successful journals are often the most profitable products of any given publisher.

Paradoxically publishers are always keen to explore the possibility of starting a new journal but, at the same time, are extremely wary of doing so. As a result, journal proposals are highly scrutinized before they are commissioned. In the first instance a commissioning editor will evaluate the proposal, using their own assessment of the market based on the experience of managing their list. They will also talk to other editors in the company, and with specialist journal staff. If they feel the idea is worth exploring they will present the proposal to a senior management committee. If this committee feels there is sufficient evidence to warrant further exploration the proposal will be sent out for review to, usually, a minimum of fifteen senior academics (often more). These reviewers will evaluate the journal concept, its potential market appeal, and the proposed editors. At any of these stages the prospective editor/editorial team might be asked to revise the proposal before proceeding to the next stage.

If the external reviews are positive and the publisher is keen to commission the journal then the commissioning editor and the publisher's journals team calculate the projected costs and earnings over a number of years and the resource allocation necessary for the journal's administration. They then set out a contract for the editor(s) that details what the publisher will do (basically manage, produce, market and distribute each issue) and what resources it will provide to the editorial team to enable them to put together each issue. In general the resource the publisher supplies is some financing. These monies are to cover the cost of editorial assistance, postage, stationery and editor expenses for trips to editorial meetings and to conferences to solicit papers. In the first few years, when the journal is establishing itself, these finances are likely to be quite meagre. If the journal is a success and attracts a number of subscriptions then the financial resourcing is likely to become more generous.

Given the financial outlay and risks associated with starting a new journal, publishers are generally looking for a proposal whose remit fills a particular niche that is not yet served by another journal, or in the case of a field that is already served by other established journals, a novel format that will have market appeal. They will also want as editors established academics whose publication record suggests that they are capable of managing a major enterprise, and whose reputation will indicate a quality product, although some publishers might take a chance on more junior academics who are on a rapid career trajectory. It is very unlikely that a publisher will commission a journal whose editors have limited publication profiles and you are almost certainly wasting your time pitching a new journal, even if your idea is an extremely good one, if you do not have an established publication record in refereed, cited journals (unless your co-editor is an established name). Other attractive features to a publisher will be a journal that has cross-disciplinary appeal and is international in scope (for example, it is aimed at an international audience and has an international mix of editors and editorial board members that would encourage adoption and submissions from these locations). Both these factors widen the potential market for subscriptions.

As with a book proposal (see Chapter 11), a journal proposal needs to cover a number of issues, such as rationale, scope, format, timing (for example, how many issues a year), market, competition and biographies of the editors. The only real difference is a section that details an (at this stage indicative) editorial board. An editorial board is a panel of 'experts' chosen to aid and guide the editor about the direction and quality of the journal. Usually board members are selected to provide a broad range of expertise. At the proposal stage the list is usually of suggested members, and might change on the advice of proposal reviewers. Only once the journal is approved are the individuals approached and signed up.

 ## Proposing a new book series

Book series are starting to become more popular with publishers. They have a number of benefits. They provide a common base and focus for organizing lists and marketing; they are good for sales as libraries are more likely to buy all the books in a series than a set of individual texts; and series are usually edited by academics who can use their networks to commission 'good' authors to produce texts, thus significantly aiding the commissioning editor. It is now becoming the case that publishers will only consider publishing research monographs within such series, for the reasons above.

All academic publishers will be receptive to receiving proposals for book series, although some prefer the format to others. What they will look for is a well-defined and coherent series that clearly claims a particular niche, has a strong projected future of titles (not a series that might potentially consist of no more than a handful of books), and has strong market potential. As with ordinary book proposals, the series will need to fit with the general publication profile of the publisher. In other words, a publisher who specializes in textbooks is likely only to consider a textbook series, and only in the subject matter it concentrates its attention on. Given the responsibility of managing a list and commissioning authors and editors, most publishers will only consider relatively experienced or established scholars as book series editors.

A book series proposal contains many of the same elements of a book proposal: rationale, scope, format, timing, market, competition and biographies of the series editor(s). It should also provide an outline of potential titles and an indicative list of authors/editors. Ideas about a common format should be detailed. Also, given that there needs to be some level of continuity between books, there should be some explanation of editorial policy. Some series employ an editorial board whose job is to review the manuscripts for quality and ensure continuity. If the series is to have a board, indicative names should be supplied. In terms of timing, the anticipated number of books to be commissioned per year should be indicated, the time period given for preparation, and an indicative date for the publication of the first book in the series.

17 EDITING A JOURNAL OR NEWSLETTER

Editing a journal or newsletter can be a challenging and demanding job. Rather than simply producing a single product, the endeavour is on-going and involves many different tasks, from liaising with authors and reviewers, soliciting copy, corresponding with the publisher, copy-editing and proofreading to maintaining accounts, and in some cases can involve typesetting, dealing with printers, distribution and processing payments. In the latter cases these are usually in-house or society enterprises that lack the production and financial backing of a publisher.

 ## Editing a journal produced by a publisher

Most leading academic journals are produced and distributed by specialist journal publishers. These are professional enterprises that are run for profit. The production of the journal is best thought of in two halves, with an academic editor dealing with one half, and a production editor employed by the publisher, the other. The academic editor (particularly in the social sciences and humanities) is essentially responsible for soliciting manuscripts, reviewing the quality of papers, liaising with authors, basic copy-editing and formatting, scheduling papers into issues, sending on material to the publishers, and proofreading the typeset manuscript (the more mechanical aspects of this list are sometimes undertaken by professional staff in the physical and natural sciences).

Given that most journals consist of four to six issues a year (and sometimes more), there are usually two or more editors, with one acting as a managing editor with overall responsibility. Sometimes, for reasons of soliciting papers and marketing, these editors represent different geographical areas or particular sub-specialties. They also usually include a specialist editor such as a book review editor. Editors are often aided by an editorial assistant who helps with tasks such as postage, chasing referees and authors, and forwarding mail to other editors. The production editor deals with the material once it has been sent to the publisher and is responsible for ensuring professional copy-editing, typesetting, collating of proofs, printing, marketing, subscriptions, distribution, financial management and indexing.

Managing an academic journal is, in some respects, like being on a treadmill. Several issues are usually in production at any one time so there is no rest period between them. At set periods, every three months for a quarterly, a book-sized manuscript has to be delivered to the publisher. Good organization is, then, the key. On taking over the editorship of an established journal you should ask the previous editor for copies of all production and financial files, details of all open papers (that is, papers that have not yet been formally accepted or rejected), and the schedule and known contents of future issues. You should also examine the management system and see if it suits how you work or whether it is the most efficient way of managing the job. One thing is certain, there *will* need to be a management system. Box 17.1 details the system for the journal *Social and Cultural Geography*, a journal with four academic editors, one of whom acts as the managing editor, and which is published six times per year.

Box 17.1 Management system for a paper submitted to the journal *Social and Cultural Geography*

1 Editorial Assistant (EA) to consult with Managing Editor for name of editor for each paper submitted.

2 EA acknowledges receipt of paper by return email, saying who the editor will be and puts preliminary details in spreadsheet – date received, author, paper title, editor.

3 EA makes the paper anonymous by stripping out contact details and then converts the file into .pdf (named with paper code., e.g. 01_04.pdf). Figures and tables are placed in separate .pdf files (e.g. 01_04_figs.pdf; 01_04_tabs.pdf).

4 EA sends the .pdf(s) to the selected editor with a request for four referees' names and their institutions (three to review, plus a reserve)

cont.

---

5   On receipt of referees' names, EA sends .pdf to referees along with an evaluation document (named as paper code, e.g. 01_04_A.doc;). Referees are given six weeks to review. If a referee does not acknowledge receipt of paper they are emailed again one week later.

6   EA updates spreadsheet with due date, referees names, etc.

7   EA makes a note in diary to remind referees one week before the paper is due.

8   EA collates the referees' comments for sending on to the editor. On receipt of a review an acknowledgement is sent.

9   EA reminds referees if needed one week after deadline (does twice, at one-week intervals, before abandoning; lets editor know if abandoned).

10 EA forwards the set of referees' comments to relevant editor.

11 EA waits two weeks and prompts the editor for a decision on the paper. Does again after another two weeks if no response.

12 Editor sends decision letter to author. This is cc'ed to EA who notes decision in spreadsheet.

Resubmitted papers

13 EA forwards the paper to the relevant editor with request as to whether the paper needs to be sent back out to none, one, two or all of the previous referees (advise which ones). Update spreadsheet that paper resubmitted.

14 If paper needs to be re-refereed, EA sends out as .pdf to relevant referee(s) (named with paper code., e.g. 01_04_rev.pdf). Referees are given four weeks to review.

15 EA updates spreadsheet with due date, referees' names, etc.

16 EA makes a note in diary to remind referees one week before the paper is due.

17 EA collates the referees' comments for sending on to editors. Acknowledge receipt of review.

18 EA reminds referees if needed one week after deadline (does twice, at one-week intervals, before abandoning; lets editor know if abandoned).

19 EA forwards the set of referees' comments to relevant editor.

cont.

20   EA waits two weeks and prompts the editor for a decision on the paper. Does again after another two weeks if no response.

21   Editor sends decision letter to author. This is cc'ed to EA who notes decision in spreadsheet.

Final papers

22   EA acknowledges receipt of final paper and provides to author approximate issue that paper will appear in. Request that the author re-checks the paper and makes sure it complies with formatting. Author to resubmit formatted paper.

23   While author formats paper, EA sends title and abstract to translators.

24   EA files final paper, plus figures and tables, in folder for submission to publisher. Rename the files to surname of first author (e.g. Kitchin_txt.doc).

25   EA adds French and Spanish abstracts to the paper.

26   Paper now ready to be submitted to publisher.

The key task of an editor is to ensure the quality of the material published in the journal. As such, the successful management of the review process is critical – selecting referees and ensuring the receipt of reviews. Perhaps the most difficult task is to evaluate the referees' reviews and to come to a decision to communicate to the author(s). In many cases, when the referees agree, it will be a relatively easy decision. However, it is not uncommon for referees to disagree, which is why employing three referees is often useful. Even so, as an editor you might still need to arbitrate. This arbitration might involve dealing with an irate author who does not like the decision made. In these cases, you should clearly state your reasoning and not allow yourself to be bullied.

 # Editing an in-house journal

Editing a journal produced by a society or department involves all of the tasks of an academic journal, minus liaising with the publisher, plus a host of other jobs. These extra jobs are those that are usually undertaken by a publisher such as typesetting, printing, marketing, distribution and account keeping. Each of these extra jobs is quite demanding and involves a range of skills. It is fair to say then that in many ways editing an in-house journal is more demanding than editing a journal produced by a publisher, which is why they often have fewer issues per year and why they are often produced by small teams, each member of which takes responsibility for different tasks.

In order to ensure an efficient operation the first thing an in-house editor needs to do is to produce a production and task schedule. The resulting timetable will detail what jobs need to be done and when. It should include the deadlines for paper submission, receipt of final papers, scheduling with printers, calculating anticipated costs, distribution, and so on (see Table 17.1). It is very important to do this advance planning to make sure that the journal appears on schedule and without making a financial loss.

Table 17.1 Production schedule of an in-house journal

Date	Action
January	Contact printers for estimate of cost
	Contact sources of subsidization and advertising for estimate of revenue
	Estimate income from subscription
	Produce a financial model for an issue [see Table 17.2]
	Call for papers with deadline
June	Deadline for receipt of papers
	Send out notice of payment to subscribers
July	Deadline for referees' reports and editor's decision
August	Contact printers and schedule production
	Process payments from subscribers
September	Deadline for resubmission of revised papers
October	Copy-edit and typeset papers
	Send proofs to authors
	Chase late payments from subscribers
November	Collate proofs
	Send manuscript to printers
December	Receive bound copies from printers
	Post finished copies to subscribers and also gratis copies

In order to ensure the journal appearing on schedule, always make sure you allow enough time for each task. As a rough estimate, one should allow a year to produce each issue. While this time lag may seem excessive it allows time to catch up if any part of the process takes longer than expected. It also takes account of the fact that editors are usually busy people, doing other jobs, and may be trying to produce a journal with multiple issues a year. In other words, issue schedules usually overlap rather than being exclusive, meaning editors are always producing two or more issues at any one time.

In-house journals are either entirely self-financing or to some degree subsidized. In both cases, though, there is a finite amount of money from which to produce the journal. A full financial model for the journal needs to be produced on the basis of anticipated sales and subsidization (see Table 17.2 on p.120). Some journals are run on a swap basis (that is, societies agree that rather than pay a fee they will swap copies of their in-house journal), meaning that the production and distribution of these issues has no source of income from subscriptions. Consequently, the subscriptions from other sales need to subsidize these costs. For in-house journals produced by a society the subscription fee might be part of a membership fee, with few other expected sales. Moreover, for all journals it is expected that the cost will reflect costs in previous years and does not wildly fluctuate. In both these cases, income is largely fixed at a certain level and the production of the journal has to stay inside these costs. This might mean keeping the journal a certain length to ensure that cost does not exceed income. Here, the only way to raise additional income is to increase the number of subscriptions or to seek revenue such as advertising.

If it is a new journal, and you are unsure of any costs, contact relevant parties (such as printers) to get quotes ahead of starting. If you are taking over the editorship of an established journal make sure all the production and financial files are passed on so you can examine past schedules and costs. Producing a Web-based journal will greatly reduce many of the costs (except if the Web design and hosting is outsourced), but not the number tasks an editor has to do.

Table 17.2 Financial model for an in-house journal

Income	
Estimated number of subscriptions	200
Gratis copies	75
Subscription fee	20
Amount of subsidization	2000
Total income	*6000*

Costs	
Estimated length of issue	100 pages
Type of binding	Stitch
Cover type	Two-colour
Paper size	A4/Letter
Paper quality	180 grams
Paper finish	Gloss
Cost per issue	15
Distribution – national (175)	Envelopes/postage (2)
Distribution – international (125)	Envelopes/postage (5)
Other costs (phone, computing, etc.)	500
Total costs	*5975*

Note: As the example is hypothetical, no currency unit has been assumed.

As for an academic journal, the editor is responsible for the quality of the content and must work with all authors to ensure that their contributions are up to the required standard.

 Editing a newsletter

Editing a newsletter involves all the same tasks as editing an in-house journal. Where it differs is in the size and scope. Newsletters are generally short publications (from one or two pages to around ten pages in length, although they can be longer) that focus on the activities of an organization and their members. Generally a newsletter serves one of two audiences – either the members of an organization, or as a marketing device aimed at those interested in the organization. In many cases it is designed to serve both. Regardless, it should be written with the intended audience in mind.

The kinds of items that usually appear in a newsletter include:

- An editorial from the newsletter editor – usually an opinion piece designed to stimulate debate or action
- Contributions from the leading members of the organization, such as the Chairperson, Treasurer, and Secretary
- Features on key pieces of work undertaken or events organized by organization members since the last newsletter
- Profiles of new members of the organization
- Awards received by organization members
- Advance notice of seminars, workshops, conferences and funding opportunities that might be of interest to readers
- Advertising – membership, conferences, jobs, goods, etc.

Lengthier and more-detailed newsletters can also take some of the formats associated with journals, including such items as book reviews, conference reports and even position pieces or polemical articles likely to be of interest to the audience.

Newsletters can be more or less formal in nature, necessitating (on the one hand) consideration of many of the issues normally associated with production of a journal (including, for example, the calculation of, and adherence to, production schedules and financial modelling), or a less stringent, and perhaps less stressful approach. Here, newsletters are normally more associated with issues surrounding self-publishing (Chapter 15), with perhaps one or two officers of any organization having responsibility for all aspects of the newsletter production and distribution process.

Increasingly, organizations are looking at ways of reducing the costs associated with production and dissemination of newsletters, while acknowledging the helpful role they play in transmitting news, and recruiting new members. As such, email dissemination, or the housing of newsletters on organization websites (with a notice of publication being sent to all members via email) are becoming increasingly popular. The latter is perhaps the best e-option as many email lists, organizations and individuals do not support or appreciate the sending of attachments because of problems with file formats, download times and viruses.

18 THE PRODUCTION PROCESS

Once an article or a book has been accepted for publication it enters the production process. Most publishers employ a production editor who will shepherd the manuscript through the many processes until final publication. Their job is to liaise between the author and the copy-editor, typesetter and printer, and to maintain a timetable. Once the book enters production it is very important to meet deadlines to ensure a timely publication. If any one stage is late the slot allocated for the next stage is missed and a new one has to be negotiated (this might be several weeks away depending on how busy the copy-editor, typesetter or printer/binder is). The production editor should supply you with a timetable for the production of your book. If it is clear that you will not be able to stick to the plan (you will be abroad attending a conference when the proofs are scheduled, for example), let them know straight away so a new timetable can be implemented before any difficulties arise.

Stages common to all publications

Book texts generally pass through two stages of production before they are published, whereas for journal articles both stages are often performed simultaneously.

◯ Copy-editing

The publisher will send a manuscript to a professional copy-editor who will check it for consistency, style, errors and omissions (whether all the references cited are in the reference list, for example). This occurs before the typesetting stage for books. Here, book authors are supplied with a list of queries to answer, usually consisting of requests for information. For journal articles, the journal editor and referees should have dealt with most substantial copy-editing relating to style and sense, so these checks are often made by a professional proofreader at a later stage (see below).

The copy-editor is employed to try to make your manuscript as readable as possible. They may well suggest some minor changes in style or that sentences or paragraphs be re-phrased. While some of their suggestions might seem petty or frustrating, they usually have good reason to forward them. While they might not be an expert on the topic being discussed, they are experienced at editing texts. If the copy-editor does not understand your sentences because they are nonsensical (rather than not understanding the content), you can be sure your audiences will not comprehend them either.

Sometimes in correcting poor English the copy-editor might inadvertently change the sense of a passage. If this is the case, rather than change it back to how it was (which was clearly problematic or it would not have been changed) rewrite it and make a polite note to the copy-editor to explain your revision. If the copy-editor makes a lot of changes or completely alters the style of a text it can be very frustrating. This is especially so if you feel your text is being over-edited and your 'voice' is being lost. If this is the case, you have the right to appeal the changes being made. This should be done diplomatically in the first instance, given that the copy-editor is trying to help. If you and the copy-editor fail to agree on the changes needed, then you should contact your commissioning editor and explain the problem.

Once copy-editing has been completed you will be sent a revised manuscript to check. In the case of a book, once you have responded to the queries the copy-edited script will be typeset before being returned.

◯ Proofing

Proofing (or proofreading) consists of checking the typeset manuscript for any errors – either minor grammatical or spelling errors not spotted by the copy-editor or flaws introduced at the typesetting stage. For journal articles that have not been through a professional copy-editing stage, there may be some queries raised by the professional proofreader at this point.

The proof stage is not an opportunity to make substantive changes to either the text or the arguments made. These should have been undertaken before final submission, and most publishers will refuse to make such changes or will charge the author the additional typesetting costs (which, if there are a lot of changes, might be substantial).

A book will almost certainly be sent out as hardcopy page proofs and changes will be handwritten on the proof set, which is posted back. Journal proofs are increasingly sent out electronically as a PDF file, with authors asked to print the proof out and post back corrections or email a list of corrections. There is a set of international proofreading symbols used to show the typesetter what changes need to be made and where. These are detailed in Figure 18.1.

Proofs are read by a professional proofreader (employed by the publisher) as well as by the author(s) and editor(s) of a collected volume or journal. All the allowable changes and typesetting corrections made by each reader will be collated by the production editor for revision by the typesetter.

● Further stages in book production

Books have a number of production tasks in addition to those experienced when publishing an article.

○ Index

Creating an index can be a demanding task and, if you wish, many publishers will employ a professional indexer to do the compiling (you will be charged for this service from your royalties). If you want to do the index yourself, the publisher will issue you with full guidelines and a template to follow. While compiling an index can be extremely tedious and time-consuming, we recommend that you do it yourself. This way you will end up with an index you think will be useful to readers (and it will save you money). The work of drawing up the entries can be done in advance but the page numbers cannot be inserted until page proof stage, when time will be limited.

○ Marketing

All publishers ask their authors to complete an author and book questionnaire to help the publisher market and sell your book. Here, you will be expected to detail the book's strengths, identify journals that might wish to review the book and recommend potential places to advertise the book's publication. You should provide as much detail as possible, but you should not oversell your case. Your book will have a set marketing budget and therefore the publisher will only send out so many copies for review. You need to make sure these copies are sent to the most appropriate journals, not a random smattering. While you might supply an extensive list, make sure you identify which journals, conferences and so on should be prioritized.

Marginal mark	Meaning	Corresponding mark in text
⟨/⟩	Leave unchanged	under characters to remain
✕	Remove extraneous marks	Encircle marks to be removed
	Change damaged character(s)	Encircle character(s) to be changed
Preceded by additional matter	Insert additional matter identified by a letter in a diamond	⋋
⌀⟋	Delete	/ or ⊢─┤ through character(s) to be deleted
⊗	Wrong fount Replace by character(s) of correct fount	Encircle character(s) to be changed
⊔	Set in or change to italic	Under character(s) to be set or changed
≡	Set in or change to capital letters	Under character(s) to be set or changed
═	Set in or change to small capital letters	Under character(s) to be set or changed
∿	Set in or change to bold type	∿∿∿ Under character(s) to be set or changed
⧧	Change capital letters to lower case letters	Encircle character(s) to be changed
⧧	Change small capital letters to lower case letters	Encircle character(s) to be changed
⊎	Change italic to upright type	Encircle character(s) to be changed
L	Substitute or insert character in 'inferior' position	/ or ⋋
⌒ e.g. ﬃ	Substitute ligature e.g. ﬃ for separate letters	⊢───┤ through character(s) affected
Write out separate letters	Substitute separate letters for ligature	⊢───┤
⅂	Substitute or insert apostrophe	/ or ⋋ where required
⅂ and / or ⅂	Substitute or insert single quotation marks	/ or ⋋ where required
⅂⅂ and / or ⅂⅂	Substitute or insert double quotation marks	/ or ⋋ where required
. . .	Substitute or insert ellipsis	/ or ⋋ where required
⊢⊣	Substitute or insert hyphen	/ through character or ⋋ where required
⊢─┤	Substitute or insert rule	/ through character or ⋋ where required
⟨/⟩	Substitute or insert oblique	/ through character or ⋋ where required
⌐	Start new paragraph	⌐
⌒	Run on (no new paragraph)	⌒
⎍⎍	Transpose characters or words	⎍⎍ between characters or words, numbered when necessary

Marginal mark	Meaning	Corresponding mark in text
1 2 3	Transpose a number of characters or words	3 2 1 | | |
─── 3 ─ ─ 2 ─── 1	Transpose a number of lines	─── 3 ─ ─ 2 ─── 1
⊏	Transpose lines	⊐
⌐⌐	Cancel indent	⊢⊏
[ ]	Centre	⌈enclosing matter⌉ ⌊to be centred ⌋
⊢─┤	Set line justified to specified measure	⊢─[and / or]─┤
⊢─┤	Set column justified to specified measure	⊢────┤
⌐	Move matter specified distance to the right	enclosing matter to be moved to the right
⌐⌐	Move matter specified distance to the left	enclosing matter to be moved to the left
⌐⌐	Raise matter	Over matter to be raised Under matter to be raised
⌐⌐	Lower matter	Over matter to be lowered Under matter to be lowered
Y	Insert space between characters	between characters affected
Y	Insert space between words	Y between words affected
⋀	Reduce space between characters	between characters affected
⋀	Reduce space between words	⋀ between words affected
Y	Make space appear equal between characters or words	between characters or words affected
(each side of column linking lines)	Close up to normal interline spacing	(each side of column linking lines)
─(or)─	Insert space between lines or paragraphs	─(or)─
⟶ or ⟵	Reduce space between lines or paragraphs	⟶ or ⟵

Figure 18.1 Standard proof correction symbols

125

Unless the book has mass-market appeal, the publisher will not try to market the book through adverts in the popular press. Instead they will rely on targeted marketing through catalogues and leaflets directed at those who work in a field. You can supplement the publisher's marketing pre- and post- publication through announcing the book's publication on relevant mailing lists, by setting up your own website that tells people about the book, including contents, author biographies, reviews and how it can be purchased (one such site is http://www.atlasofcyberspace.com/), and by presenting the book's argument at conferences and seminars.

○ Book cover

Either an in-house or a specifically commissioned designer usually produces the book cover. You are, however, entitled to make suggestions. If you want to use a particular picture you might need to secure copyright permission. The publisher covers the cost of producing the cover and they might veto your idea if it is too expensive. Always ask to see the draft cover when it is being designed to check that you like it and that all the details are correct (from experience it is surprising how many mistakes arise). Some publishers do not do this automatically and many authors first see the cover when they get bound copies.

○ Timing

From delivery of the manuscript until the book hits the bookshop shelves is usually around forty weeks. This might seem like a long time but the manuscript has to pass through several stages, only a few of which the author is actively involved in. Once the text has been checked, then sent to a copyeditor, typeset and proofed, it has to be manufactured and pre-publication marketing stepped up. Manufacture itself is a complex process involving many suppliers and contractors. Each stage also necessitates checking for quality by the publisher before the next is sanctioned. In addition, some publishers like to release books at a set date to coincide with a new academic semester/year or the production of a new catalogue. They might then hold back the launch of a book until that date. Remember an important part of the book is how it is presented and marketed, not simply its content. The publisher will supply you with an estimated date of publication. If the book has not been published within four weeks of this date, contact either the commissioning or production editor for an update.

After publication

Once a book is published the relationship with the publisher and the book is not over. The book has to be marketed and sold (and payments received!). As noted above, you can enhance your sales through your own efforts. If the book has sold particularly well the publisher will reprint the book. There is an opportunity at this point to correct any minor errors that have been spotted since publication. If after a few years the book is still selling, the publisher might ask you to consider writing a second edition. The benefit of writing such a text is that the work should be less in that it consists of updating an existing text, the financial return is known, and you can respond to reviewers' comments.

 ## A final word

Remember, as a contracted author you have rights. If you are not happy with the production process you should talk to either the commissioning editor or the production editor.

19 ATTENDING CONFERENCES AND PRESENTING PAPERS AND POSTERS

This chapter focuses on issues associated with attending, and presenting at, events at which research is disseminated to a live audience. In particular, we consider how to decide which events to attend, and how best to present your material (either in academic paper or poster form). The term conference in the chapter title is therefore used as a surrogate for other 'live' events such as seminars, symposia, colloquia, workshops and plenaries. A *seminar* is usually an event where there is only one speaker presenting. They are usually organized as part of an academic department's activities, with the audience usually being limited to faculty and students within an institution. A *colloquium* is a set of seminars on a common theme, usually spread over a few weeks. A *symposium* consists of only three or four invited speakers, each of whom presents on a related topic. A *workshop* usually involves short presentations designed to be foils that stimulate debate and group sessions where issues are discussed among the delegates. A *plenary* is a special session at a conference where a guest lecturer speaks to delegates. It is usual that no other conference activities occur at this time. A *conference* has many speakers, often organized into sessions. Participation is open, in that anyone who wants to present can apply to do so. In some cases, everyone who wants to speak is given a slot, in other cases slots are allocated on a competitive basis (selected through a refereeing process).

Which event(s) to attend?

As suggested above, in any one academic year there is a wide range of different types of event one can attend. These may be discipline-specific, be regularly organized or annual events (for example, as organized by national societies or organizations), or they may be more general, cross-disciplinary, and 'of the moment', issue-based gatherings. Your decision concerning which to attend of course presumes that you have knowledge of all the events that might be potentially interesting or advantageous to attend (in that you might meet or hear speak researchers whose work you admire) at any one time. Unfortunately this is often not the case, and it is surprising how often you decide to attend one event, commit resources and plan accordingly, only for another to come over the horizon that perhaps might have been even better.

Fortunately, most of the larger conferences will be some time in their planning and marketing, allowing you to plan attendance well in advance. Most others will be advertised nine months to a year in advance to allow for the call of papers and for the organizers to prepare everything. This lead-in time is not just important to organizers but also to attendees.

Given that the resources made available to academics for conference attendance seems to be getting increasingly hard to come by, selecting events to attend necessitates careful thought and planning. Often the events you choose to attend will depend on the stage in your career and which publication strategy you are employing. For instance, and as noted in Chapter 2, if you are a postgraduate student then you are perhaps best focusing on those events where a supportive environment for postgraduate students will be most forthcoming (such as postgraduate-only conferences, smaller regional and specialist conferences, and postgraduate sessions at major conferences). This might be especially the case if you are presenting material. If you are employed on a contract post then you might want to attend conferences where potential future employers might be. If you are seeking tenure then maybe you will need to attend national disciplinary or international events, and so on. So, find the right audience for your publication strategy, considering whether this might be found at more specialist, rather than generic gatherings, outside your discipline, and/or at local, regional, national or international events. You might also consider where the best place is to meet people interested in your field (or simply to visit!).

We have already alluded to the fact that the ability to choose which event to attend is increasingly more a question of which one conference to attend per year, as resources available to many academics are being cut, while simultaneously the costs of attendance are seemingly on the increase. Conferences are now a mini-industry for many institutions and organizations, and fees and costs can be extremely expensive, if not exclusionary.

This is not always the case, however, depending on the rationale behind the event, its main aims, whether it is being sponsored or funded in some other way, and so on. Indeed some events simply look to cover their costs, which they seek to keep to a minimum (for example, the two-day conference discussed in the Preface cost delegates £30 ($45), with reduced costs for postgraduates, many of whom also received bursaries; also see Chapter 21).

Some or all of the costs of attendance can be met (or alleviated) in four ways. First, institutions usually have a 'staff development' or research/conference fund that can be applied to (though in many cases these funds have shrunk significantly in recent years and are likely only to cover some basic costs and rarely the full amount). Second, there might be bursaries available from conference organizers, usually aimed at helping postgraduate students attend (or provided by another group and coordinated through the conference). Third, there might be monies allocated to conference attendance through research grants or awards. Fourth, you can seek to minimize your own costs by not purchasing the full conference package. For example, paying the registration fees (perhaps just for the day you are presenting on) and using alternative cheaper accommodation, dealing with one's own catering needs, and so on. This can be less convenient and perhaps less social, but it will certainly be a lot cheaper!

 ## Deciding whether to participate/organize a session

On deciding which events to attend, it is also necessary to decide the extent to which you will participate in the event by presenting your work or organizing a session. In some cases such participation will not be possible, because these options are restricted by the event organizers (usually the case with seminars, workshops and symposia). In other cases, our advice is to seek to present whenever an opportunity arises and you have something you feel is worth saying. Events are great venues to try out and share new ideas and findings, to discuss work in progress and get feedback on papers ahead of submitting them to a journal. You should note that in many institutions monies towards attendance are often conditional on presenting.

Very large conferences often stream presentations into sessions, where papers on a similar topic are grouped together, while posters are organized and grouped together irrespective of focus. The conference organizers will do this streaming, but often they will also allow delegates to self-organize themselves into sessions. The benefit of being in one of these sessions is that someone has gone through the trouble of creating a session on a specific theme, rather than papers being lumped together.

An option might be for you to organize a session(s) if there is a particular theme that you feel would benefit from a concentrated examination. Before advertising for submissions, the conference organizers should be contacted to make sure they are happy for you to organize a session on a particular theme. Once they have approved the session it can be advertised via mailing lists or you could contact specialists direct to see whether they would like to participate. If you receive a large number of interested enquiries you will either need to expand the number of sessions you organize or have to select which papers to include or exclude. Once the sessions are finalized all the necessary material will need to be forwarded to the conference organizers. The main benefit of organizing a session is that you can bring papers together on a topic of interest to you, but you do not have the hassle of organizing the full event (and having to deal with room hire, registration, catering, accommodation, etc.).

 ## Organizing your attendance

For the larger, more expensive conferences, and especially those that are overseas from your location, you should not underestimate the amount of time it can take to organize all the different practical aspects of your trip. Once you have decided how long you are attending for (and whether you are going to supplement this time with doing something else at the conference location), you will need to consider how you are going to get there, and where you are going to stay (in any conference-linked accommodation or find your own room). If you are lucky you may have the ability to call on help from within your own department or institution in planning your travel (and increasingly this is a requirement as institutions often have agreements with local service and travel providers). It is often best to specify a few options that are favourable to you, and then see what is identified by the institutional support. If you are self-organizing, then a good Internet travel site or travel agent will provide a range of options to suit your needs.

There are all the usual issues associated with overseas travel to be aware of – acquiring all the relevant travel documents (such as ensuring your passport is up to date, and that you have satisfied the necessary visa requirements), insurance or medical certificates, obtaining local currency in advance of your trip, getting to the airport or railway station on time, and so on – but additionally you have to ensure all materials in relation to your conference attendance and/or presentation are traveling with you! Moreover, you may need to be aware of issues such as the potential effects of jet lag and the negative impact that might have (arriving the night before a morning presentation is usually a bad idea).

Presenting a paper

Although many academics are actively involved in the presentation of material to undergraduate and postgraduate students as part of their academic duties, the thought of talking in front of an audience of academic peers still often causes considerable anxiety. In such a situation, most of us are nervous and apprehensive to some degree, and fear of potential embarrassment is entirely normal – few people have the natural confidence and oratory skills needed to captivate an audience. Those who do, have often put in a lot of work and practice to do so. Presenting a talk to other people is a skill that can be learned, which develops with experience, but which is underscored by a commitment to always being as well prepared as possible.

Presentations and fear

According to Uncommon Knowledge (www.uncommon-knowledge.co.uk), the top ten fears surrounding presentations are as follows:

1   'Drying up' or not being able to speak
2   Forgetting what you are talking about – your mind going blank
3   Having the 'heckler from hell'
4   Having someone in the audience who knows more than you do
5   People noticing you are nervous
6   Having to run screaming from the room
7   The presentation being so awful and embarrassing that your social/career relationships are forever ruined
8   The impossible to answer 'question from hell'
9   The audience talking over you or walking out
10   'Dying on stage'

This list certainly strikes a chord concerning the types of fear that develop as a presentation (that you signed up to six months ago) draws closer. However, feeling anxious is to a certain degree a good thing as it improves memory, provides more energy and makes us more dynamic. The secret to keeping these fears in check is preparation: if the presentation is well prepared and rehearsed then everything should go well.

○ Be prepared

While we all might admire the ability of those who can deliver a relevant and resonant, humorous, well-structured and beautifully delivered presentation that was guided by a few scribbled notes on the back of an envelope written five minutes before the presentation, the reality for most of us is that the better prepared you are, the more familiar you are with your material, the more comfortable and confident you (should) feel. Undoubtedly you might make a few minor changes to your work on listening to other presentations, or the audience comments, but on the whole your presentation should be fully complete, and rehearsed well in advance of the event. In short, you need to know the *content* of your presentation, and how it is going to be *presented*, inside out.

○ Presentation content and structure

In many ways the content of the presentation can be likened to the steps taken in writing a journal article (see Chapter 6). Like an article, the presentation requires a clear structure and strong narrative flow, with a clear beginning, middle and end. Indeed, because any presentation is 'of the moment' (for example, as an audience member you cannot 're-read' any part of a presentation you do not immediately understand), it is important that you help your audience follow your line of argument(s) and the logic of your work, or else they may become lost and disinterested.

While it is not normally required, you may find it useful to produce a full written paper to accompany your presentation, from which the main aspects of your talk will be drawn. This allows you to fully focus your work, as you would do for a written article. However, it also provides those in attendance with something to take away (and cite!), as well as allowing for feedback on an early draft of a potentially revised and submitted journal article.

Make sure the material you present is thoroughly researched. Depending on the nature of the talk it will need a balance of argument and evidence, and you should attempt to avoid cramming in too many facts, or simply too much information. In general terms two or three main points is sufficient, linked to the themes of the conference (and or session), and pitched at the correct level according to the audience you expect to be presenting to. Remember you have limited time available, and are unlikely to be able to convey the level of detail you would like, or deem necessary. However, in many ways that is not what is required – what you need to do is to be as pertinent and concise as possible, while allowing your audience to follow your line of enquiry, understand your arguments, appreciate your conclusions, and become hungry for more! As such, you should avoid getting too technical or theoretical (the level of detail included in your talk clearly depends on your audience and their capacity to receive and understand, but in general terms too much detail delivered too quickly will quickly alienate any audience). You want to show your audience that you understand what you are talking about, and the best way of doing this is to translate difficult concepts or terminology from their original form or language into something understandable (and interesting). In essence, you should aim to impress by making things less complicated than they are in reality, not more so!

◯ Presentation design

No matter how good any written version of your presentation is, if it is poorly presented it will be remembered for all the wrong reasons. A key aspect here is the preparation of accompanying material.

Accompanying material usually refers to visual aids such as overheads containing bullet points, pieces of text, tables, figures and so on or slides, but can also refer to music and video. Visual aids can help to illustrate your thesis and keep the audience interested. If presenting text, it is important to strike a balance between presenting too much detail (in too small a font) and too little so that its use is almost meaningless. Experience suggests that, at the very least, you should try to summarize visually the main points of your talk. Text should be at least size 24 point to be visible from the back of a room. Illustrations should be used where appropriate, with all figures, tables and maps presented professionally. It is also important to remember that there may be audience members who are (partially) deaf and who might be relying on your overheads and your lips to understand your talk.

An increasingly popular choice for presenters is to use Microsoft PowerPoint (part of Microsoft Office). On a basic level, PowerPoint is essentially a fancy form of overheads which allows the use of different backgrounds, colour and pictures, and is presented using a 'slide-show' format. It can be used more imaginatively however to include video clips, sound links and moving text. Of course such 'innovations' can help to keep an audience interested. They should be used in moderation, however, as flying text (in particular) can quickly become rather distracting (and you should remember it is the meaning of the text you are trying to convey, not that you have mastered PowerPoint!). Further, be aware that facilities available at conferences may not match your own technology (although it can often be much better!). This might lead to, at best, a slower than normal 'slide-show', or, at worse, an inability to access or run the necessary file. Indeed, the latter is the biggest weakness concerning the use of PowerPoint – the reliance on technology (the computer, the projectors, the disk, etc.). Our recommendation is to always enquire about the resources at your disposal prior to an event, check the suitability of the technology as soon as you can once you have arrived, and have at least one back-up plan (normally acetate overheads) just in case. There is nothing worse than travelling a long way at great cost to not be able to deliver your talk as hoped.

Another key aspect of the presentation design concerns length. Much like being able to convey any written message within a certain word length, you must be able to deliver your verbal and visual message in the time made available to you. It is self-centred and unprofessional to run over time when presenting your work. It appears that you are unprepared and has the potential to incur the wrath of the session or conference conveners, annoy your audience, and impact negatively on someone else's presentation. Most conference sessions are carefully scheduled, with limited additional time made available. If you do think your work is important, ensure your presentation is so effective that people will either want to talk to you afterwards, or will want to read more if paper copies are available.

◯ Presentation rehearsal

With your talk designed, you now need to practise. Practise presenting your talk out loud, using whatever aids you will use at the presentation, keeping to any time limit. If necessary get a friend, or family member, to listen to what you have to say. If it needs to be revised, either to hone content or to make it shorter, do the necessary changes and then run through it again to ensure the corrections have worked. Then rehearse it again, and again. Practice is the key, not least so that you know your material thoroughly, but also so you are comfortable with those aspects that are not directly relevant to the talk so that you can field related questions if necessary. Indeed, you should also think carefully about how people might challenge your ideas and why, and prepare suitable answers.

⭘ On the day

Always arrive a little early at the venue and make sure any equipment you require (overhead/slide/data projector, for example) is present, that it works and that you know how to use it. You should introduce yourself to the chair of the session in advance, confirm how the session will operate and that the time slot for your talk has not changed.

The key aspects of delivering your paper are as follows:

- *Breathe and relax*   When it is your turn, attempt to relax. If your talk has been well prepared, and extensively practised, all should go well. Vary the tone of your voice, speak clearly, but not too quickly – sometimes the latter aspect can be hard to achieve due to fear, or the adrenalin pumping through you! However, you need to breathe at some point, so use these natural breaks (which hopefully correspond to a grammatically well-constructed paper or set of notes or the changing of visual aids) as an opportunity to pause at relevant or strategic junctures. This will enhance the audience's consumption of your main points.
- *Eye contact*   Your audience is more likely to pay attention, and look back at you, if they think you are watching them! If you are not comfortable looking the audience in the eye (just in case they look bored, start frowning, laughing and so on), either pick out one or two apparently hooked or sympathetic audience members and focus on them, or speak to the spaces between audience members. Verbalize everything that is on your overheads – there might be people present who are visually impaired. However, do not speak directly at your overheads or the screen, as the projection of your voice will be lost.
- *Enthuse your audience*   Remember, if you appear unable to get excited by your work, or appear bored, why should your audience be any different? Much of this concerns your personal demeanour – how you

look, the way you stand, how interested (and interesting) you appear, and the degree to which you interact with your audience as you attempt to draw them into your work.

- *Be prepared to answer questions at the end of the talk*   Listen to each question carefully. If you do not understand the question or do not know the answer, do not panic, be truthful and ask the enquirer to repeat their question or say that you are sorry but you do not know the answer. Saying that you are unsure of the answer is preferable to making something up and then looking a fool when it is exposed. You should be prepared to defend your work from criticism (especially if you have critiqued a theory or approach).

Presenting a poster

While presenting a poster at an event entails many of the same aspects as presenting your work in an oral form, poster presentations are in some ways more challenging in that you have to depend on the visual and written impact alone. As such, the material you present has to 'speak' for you (almost as if you are presenting an oral paper through the use of PowerPoint slides alone).

Why use a poster?

You may wish to produce and display a poster for a number of reasons. A key reason might relate to the stage you are at in your career, and the publication strategy you are pursuing. As noted in Chapter 1, certain events might be considered more appropriate, or easier going, for the novice academic. Here, the production and dissemination of a poster might be considered to be an easier option, a less stressful way of presenting material – following the preparation stage, and once the poster is in place, what else is there for one to do? However, as we will see, far from being stress-free, poster dissemination has its own 'rules' that need to be adhered to, and pitfalls to avoid, before any semblance of peaceful (or even absentee) presentation can ensue.

Other reasons to produce a poster might include a perception that such visual display is more immediate and has a greater impact than an oral presentation. It might be that the material being presented is perceived to work more effectively in a visual form, presenting text and graphics that can be read at leisure that would be difficult to describe orally. It might also be the case that the presenting slots were full, or that you wanted to present your work at the conference but could not attend due to cost or other commitments (in which case the poster is sent to the organizers in advance). As with any other form of dissemination, posters are an opportunity to sell yourself and your work, or an opportunity to network (at least your name, if not your face).

Whatever the main reason for producing a poster, there are a number of key aspects that need to be addressed in order for your work to receive the reception you would wish.

○ **Key features of producing and presenting a poster**

As with many written forms of publication, the main points to consider in designing your poster concern its content, structure and overall design (including visual impact).

The preparation of the content of the poster can be likened to that for an oral presentation (and journal article) – and like these other forms, the time needed should not be under-estimated. In order for your poster to have the necessary clear structure, strong narrative and visual flow (leading the viewer through the material presented in a clear and logical manner), multiple edits and reviews will almost certainly be necessary. Here, again, it may be helpful to produce a full written paper to accompany your presentation, from which the main aspects of your poster are drawn. If favoured, posters can also be more abstract, relying solely on visual impact to convey your message(s), and letting the viewer take their own route around the contents and derive their own perception of your production. However, if this route is chosen you should perhaps be prepared for your work to be interpreted in ways very different from what you imagined, and/or hoped.

In practical terms, the preparation stage should include researching the requirements and logistics of the event in which your poster will be presented. You should, for example, clearly identify how much space you will have, how your poster will be displayed, whether you will require your own methods of fastening the poster to whatever surface is provided, and whether you are expected to be in attendance.

Design-wise, as with oral papers, you should ensure your material is thoroughly researched, whist avoiding cramming too much information onto the display area. You should bear in mind that any potential 'viewer' needs to be encouraged to look at your submission, and this interest needs to be sustained if you wish them to receive all of your message(s). Perhaps the easiest way of ensuring this is to draw on the services of a dedicated and specialist designer. Many institutions now have such reprographic and design services in-house, meaning that there may well be a high degree of expertise for you to draw upon locally. The extent to which you (can) do this, however, will probably be related to the resources at your disposal. The answer to this question may also impact on such issues as the type of board used to display your work, whether the poster is produced in colour, whether you get the finished article laminated, and so on.

Whether you have help to draw upon or not, there are a few key 'rules' to successful poster dissemination (that seemingly belie its reputation as an easy option!):

- Keep the text to a minimum – it is a poster after all, not the written paper pasted to a board (or at least it shouldn't be!).
- Try to keep the material, and your message, simple – write concisely, use the space available, and be selective, as you will be unable to say all you want to say. You might want to provide a handout, however, or more detailed commentary for people to take away with them.
- Give your work a recognizable structure, utilizing such sections as title, summary, introduction, methodology, results and conclusions.
- Avoid getting too technical or theoretical (with the level of detail again dependent on the intended audience), although there is perhaps a little more scope for reflection and thought on the part of the (albeit a dedicated) viewer than there is within the usual time-constrained paper presentation format.
- Avoid using different fonts (styles of lettering) on the same poster, striving instead to hold to the same style throughout.
- Ensure titles are not too small, being instead visible from a distance, and avoid the use of repetitive upper-case lettering.
- Always spell-check your final text and ensure it is grammatically correct.
- Try to cut back on words by utilizing drawings, pictures, graphs and so on whenever possible – ultimately, however, there should be a balance of text and graphics (pictures only speak for themselves to a certain degree).
- While you want your work to catch the eye, your use of colours should also attempt to be relatively tasteful, if not pleasing on the eye.

- You should be mindful of how people read – usually from top left to bottom right, and consider using columns, spaces, or directional markers to ensure the reader moves logically through your work as you would like them too.
- Ensure your audience knows who you are, and where they can contact you if necessary – posters are a good form of introduction and networking (see Chapter 20), so consider leaving business cards, and/or a comments and contact sheet. This is particularly the case if you will not be accompanying your display in person.
- Many poster presentation sessions require the author to be present, at least at specified times. You should therefore be fully comfortable with discussing your material. It is a good idea to have perfected and practised a 3–5 minute explanation of your work for delivery to those who stop and ask a question.
- To get them to stop at your poster, however, rather than just hurry past, you should also be mindful of your own visual presentation! Failure to smile, and/or look interested could easily impact negatively on any work, no matter the quality.

A good way of thinking through poster design is to look at the posters of colleagues, which are often displayed in the corridors of university departments, or to browse poster displays at conferences. You will get an idea as to which posters you think 'work' and those that don't. Borrow the ideas from those that 'work' and do not use the excuse of the precedent of poor designs to justify your own!

REFERENCES
Uncommon Knowledge http://www.uncommon-knowledge.co.uk/public_speaking.html. Last accessed 4 August 2004.

20 MAKING AND KEEPING CONTACTS

An important aspect of publicising research concerns the dissemination of your 'self' – who you are, what you do, what you stand for and so on. Much of this might be considered simply to be about being active, getting/being seen, building a reputation and image, and so on. However, and as the title of this chapter implies, there is more to this than a scatter-gun, one-way flow of (self-propelled) information in the hope that some of it sticks and contacts are made – it is about *keeping* contacts as well as making them in the first place. You may be highly successful in promoting yourself; however, if the message that is received by others is not received well, you will find that few people will remember you, or more importantly, you may well be remembered for all the wrong reasons. In this chapter therefore we approach the issue of 'making and keeping contacts' with a more expansive vision, moving beyond an individualistic, self-interested outlook on self-promotion. We begin by briefly discussing how and why we might want to network, before moving to consider the practical aspects – the things we can do.

Networking

> Networking consists of creating links from people we know to people they know in an organized way, for a specific purpose, while remaining committed to doing our part and expecting nothing in return. (Fisher and Vilas, 1996: 14)

There is a number of reasons why you should want to make and keep contacts. Most obviously, successful networking provides many benefits. You become part of a wider community, develop an (hopefully beneficial) image and reputation, and become able to draw on the support and help from others in that community (or at least find comfort in knowing where to look for that support if it is ever needed). Alternatively, it may be that in becoming part of a wider community, you become the source of support and help for others.

Practically, networking can also help you achieve goals that are related to, and framed within, whatever approach to publication you identify for yourself in Chapter 2. Networking can be used strategically in a number of ways. For example, it will help to build your academic, and/or research profile, through your work becoming known to conference organizers, journal and book editors, and so on, who may seek you out in future rather than leaving you to do the chasing. It may help you to secure a job or meet potential employers. It might also enhance your research and publication profile through collaborative research and writing, perhaps allowing you to 'jump scale' beyond your supposed level of academic standing by working with others more experienced than you (or again, to work with others with less experience).

Clearly, there are many benefits to be gained from the making and keeping of contacts. However, there are different ways in which this task can be both approached and achieved. In their work *Successful Networking*, Fisher and Vilas distinguish between making and keeping contacts as a 'thing to do' on the one hand, and as an attitude, 'an approach to life', encompassing 'the way in which you relate to the people and the resources around you' on the other (1996: 2). According to them, the latter 'creates a power that leads to a richer, fuller personal and professional life . . . a power that comes from a spirit of giving and sharing'. While perhaps being somewhat utopian in essence, the desire behind these words does seemingly have links to our goals in this volume, of making life easier for academics, while also working within (and seeking to unsettle) the oppressive accountancy structures and work practices that increasingly strive to set disciplinary colleagues against one another, increasing competition between academics as *individuals* (even within the same departments and institutions, let alone between them). At the very least, Fisher and Vilas raise important questions about how we conduct ourselves within our disciplines, and the potential benefits that might be achieved by a more collective, almost altruistic approach to our colleagues. Moreover, while their focus is clearly participants in the world of business rather than education, the principles underlying successful networking in these two spheres appear to be very similar. Let us look at their ideas in more detail.

From independence to inter-dependence

The biggest barrier to successful networking, according to Fisher and Vilas, concerns what they call the 'Lone Ranger mentality' – the idea that within Western culture we can/should accomplish tasks with little difficulty (no matter what they are) in an *independent* manner without the need for assistance (as asking for assistance is seen as tantamount to an expression of personal weakness). In order to surmount this obstacle, a different vision is required – one of *inter*-dependence. This is centred on interactions, relations and opportunities, while emphasizing the importance of trust, relationship and respect. Hence, networking moves beyond an individualistic exercise towards a *collective* process of giving and receiving information for the *mutual* benefit of everyone comprising any network of contacts.

This all sounds very appealing and simple. However, and as Fisher and Vilas emphasize, the move from independence to inter-dependence requires allaying a number of (often deep-rooted) fears:

- Rejection – only becomes an issue if you require a particular response (from a particular person); if the aim is more open and less directed, any response is welcome and beneficial.
- Obligation – only becomes an issue if your network is shallow and members are 'keeping score' of contributions; in a mutually supporting network, there are no expectations and/or obligations, only respect and appreciation.
- Appearing weak or needy – when asked for help, we feel pleased, acknowledged, even honoured, so why fear others will feel differently?
- Not having enough time – this presumes that networking is another thing to do, rather than being a way of helping with the things that need to be done.

With such fears allayed, networking moves beyond a focus on you as an individual, and what you can get by selling yourself, towards a broader vision of

> results *and* relationships; effectiveness *and* efficiency; assertiveness *and* graciousness; persistence *and* trusting; promoting yourself *and* promoting others; building your business *and* enhancing your life; receiving *and* giving; accepting support *and* contributing; [and] requesting *and* offering'
> (Fisher and Vilas 1996: 29).

Of course, the growth of academic capitalism and competitive, corporate educational environments puts such collective aspirations under pressure, although ironically funding agencies have become keen on fostering networks as a way of creating critical mass and scaling up competition in the knowledge economy at a global scale (for example, the EU versus the US). In our opinion, you will receive a lot more from networking through nurturing inter-dependent relationships than seeking to exploit them for your own gain.

Successful networking – the practicalities

A wide and varied range of actants (people, processes, things) contributes to the process of networking, many of which are examined in more detail in other chapters. These include attending and/or organizing conferences, presenting papers, courting publishers, teaching, phone calls, travel, emails, web-pages, books, activism, mailing lists, e-fora, discussion groups, reading groups, professional organizations, business cards, speeches, pamphleteering, lectures, workshops, seminars, research groups, parties, grapevines, mutual friends, summit meetings, coalitions, tapes and newsletters (adapted from Ferguson, 1981, cited in Fisher and Vilas, 1996: 30–31). All of these conduits offer potential beneficial interactions and help to nurture and sustain networks. While long-distance and virtual interactions do lead to rich interactions, there is no substitute for actual face-to-face meetings, which is why travelling to events and taking part in conferences (including their social aspects) is so important.

As emphasized in the first part of this chapter, in order for any networking to be successful, and to enhance your ability to make and keep contacts, the various elements have to be approached and interacted with in the right way. Fisher and Vilas present a number of secrets for successful networking, which seek to combine the practical elements within a mutual, supportive vision – more than just something to do. Some of these secrets are listed in Box 20.1.

Box 20.1 Secrets of successful networking

- Be clear about your expertise and the resource you can be for others.
- Have a written list of long- and short-term goals that you renew and revise regularly.
- Introduce yourself in a way that is clear, concise and personable, and that generates interest.
- Reintroduce yourself to people rather than waiting for them to remember you.
- Focus on people as they are introduced to you so that you remember their name and who they are.
- Become comfortable promoting and creating visibility for yourself.
- Be gracious and courteous with everyone you meet.
- Have sufficient business cards handy for each situation and give out your business cards appropriately.
- Acknowledge the people who inspire you, whether or not you personally know them.
- Graciously receive and accept acknowledgement and support.
- Establish an effective system for organizing and retrieving your network.
- Return phone calls within twenty-four hours.
- Organize your thoughts before making a phone call to referrals, leads or people in your network.
- Say no to events, activities and meetings that drain your time, energy or focus.
- Make requests of your network in a clear, concise and non-demanding manner.
- Follow up promptly on leads.
- Become a member of a professional organization.
- Serve on a committee or board of an organization.
- Be aware of and use the 'three foot rule' – 'anyone who is within three feet of you is a potential candidate for conversation and networking'.
- Become committed to the success of the people in your network.
- Operate with integrity and professionalism in all your interactions and endeavours.

Source: Fisher and Vilas, 1996

These secrets, we would argue, have some degree of value to add to the pursuit of successful self-publication in the long term. In terms of building academic networks, alongside attending and organizing events, taking an active role in professional organizations and becoming a steward for your discipline/field will open useful networks and demonstrate your commitment to them. More than that, however, in an academic world increasingly characterized by misguided beliefs in the benefits of market-driven competition designed to set institution against institution, academic against academic, a more collective and inclusionary vision of where we all sit in relation to our departmental, institutional, disciplinary colleagues may serve both to help us survive the pressures of day-to-day academic life while also enhancing the potential for these approaches to be collectively critiqued, destabilized and ultimately replaced with less exploitative ways of working.

REFERENCES
Fisher, D. and Vilas, S. (1996) *Successful Networking: The Key to Personal and Professional Success.* London: Thorsons.

21 ORGANIZING EVENTS

While often complex and stressful, event organization can be a highly rewarding form of publicity. Events can take many shapes and forms, from the one-hour in-house seminar, to the week-long, international conference. The impulse behind their organization can also be equally wide and varied. Organizers may be seeking to raise money, or to raise the profile of a particular department, institution, or academic field. Alternatively, their motives might be either to reflect or direct new ideas in a particular area of academic interest, perhaps seeking to solidify their place in history as being where x, y and z came together to discuss *that* issue, or where *that* publication emanated from. It might just be, however, that events remain in the memory for longest because of who was there, and what was talked about (and often away from the event venue).

Whatever the motive, however, it is fair to say that there is often little critical reflection on the ways in which academic events are organized. In particular, all such events are saturated with power relations and taken-for-granted norms. This being the case, alongside providing practical advice on how to organize events, in this chapter we highlight some of these norms and how they can be destabilized and challenged in order to make academic events more inclusive in nature. These extra suggestions are not particularly onerous or expensive to implement, and yet they can transform events from being mundane, repetitive and/or simply exploitative, towards being genuinely friendly, interactive, stimulating and rewarding.

Event planning

Although events can pass very quickly (an afternoon, a few days . . .), they can take an inordinate amount of time to plan and organize. For example, for a reasonably sized event (such as, say, a conference with around 100 people attending, over two or three days), a period of at least twelve months might be considered to be the minimum amount of time required between the initial planning stages and the event taking place (and often this will be much longer, certainly for very large conferences). Whatever the event, however, the basic rule is that the timescale should never be underestimated.

The time it takes to organize an event is, of course, related to whether you are organizing it in isolation or with colleagues. In general, most events (and prospective event organizers!) require, or substantially benefit from, the dedication of multiple co-organizers, particularly in terms of being able to draw upon their assistance through the allocation and sharing of specific (and necessary) tasks/jobs. Two examples of this approach include: the British Society of Criminology Conference, where, while being hosted by a specific institution (the University of Portsmouth in 2004), individual conference streams (representing the main conference themes) were coordinated by an individual staff member at that institution who had responsibility for organizing sessions, panels, papers and so on for their stream; and the European Social Science History Conference (ESSHC), where ideas, plans for sessions, and the final presentation of papers are coordinated by the Chair(s) of one of a large number of 'networks', each of which covers a particular topic. Both examples embody a fairly visible form of the sharing of the event-planning burden; often such support can be more hidden and/or (un) acknowledged.

While such help is undoubtedly beneficial, it is still necessary for one or two people to take overall responsibility for the whole organization process, not least in terms of taking a central role in developing and enforcing a timetable of tasks to be done by a certain date (perhaps so that any (self) imposed deadlines stand a chance of being met), or in having a close eye on budgets.

 Budgets/costs

Whatever type or style of event you choose to organize, the event organizer(s) should construct (and keep updated) a detailed budget that identifies all projected costs and income. Whether the main aim of the event is to raise money or not, most organizers would probably want (if not need) the event to break even, and it is all too easy for spending to spiral out of control. Further, most costs tend to be identifiable (and fixable)

during the planning stages and so may impact on the decisions made at this time. Some costs tend to be unavoidable, or core costs; others can be disconnected from the main 'conference fee', even though participants ultimately have to pay what is due (though to a level of their, rather than the conference organizer's choosing). In general, you should attempt to obtain information and costings from a number of service providers although you might be somewhat hamstrung by in-house agreements concerning who should provide services such as on-campus catering.

As noted above, conferences, seminars and workshops are now often seen as income-generating events. Their primary function, however, remains the dissemination and debate of new knowledge and ideas. To maintain that function they have to be accessible to the intended audience. If the intended audience is academics and postgraduates on limited budgets then this means keeping the cost as low as possible. In particular, there should be reduced costs for postgraduate students, unemployed and retired delegates. Where possible, bursaries should be given to postgraduates to offset their costs. Many professional organizations will provide these bursaries if the conference is linked to them in some way (as a form of 'sponsorship'). Of course the key phrase above is 'intended audience': it is possible to arrange events that are very cheap to attend, mainly by cutting down on the 'frills' found at many conferences (glossy programmes, conference bag of 'freebies', and so on) but also by giving some attention to such core issues as event catering and accommodation (see below).

It is important to make sure that you know who payment should be payable to and in what form your organization is able to accept payment. You should also know the procedure for paying for services in advance of receiving attendance fees. Make sure that only one person is responsible for managing the finances.

 Event focus/goal/purpose

Event planning and budgeting substantially benefits from the organizer(s) having a clear understanding of the proposed event's (main) focus/goal from the outset – that is, what you, as organizer(s), want to achieve by holding the event. For example, the event might primarily be to provide a service to those interested in that topic or to raise the profile of a particular group, or institution, as a form of publicity. Its main function could be to generate new ideas, and/or reflect or steer a 'new direction' in a discipline, or perhaps it might be envisaged (at the initial planning stages at least!) to do all of these things.

Whatever the specific aim, having a clear idea of what it is can often help in steering decisions relating to other aspects of organizing the event. For example, the scale/size and format of any event can be affected by the breadth or narrowness of the event's focus and potential 'audience appeal'. For example, an event that is relatively narrow in scope, or is perhaps issue-specific, may (self-)limit the number of attendees (although obviously it depends what that single issue is). Alternatively, the event might encompass a broad and potentially rather disparate range of topics and themes (such as national or international disciplinary meetings), meaning that a wide range of interested parties could potentially attend.

Event length and scheduling

The length of the entire proposed event can itself vary from as little as one morning or afternoon, to multiple days. When thinking about how long you want your event to last you should consider how the length would affect potential participants' ability to attend. This might be as a result of the distance from the venue, the time it would take to get there, the cost to be incurred, or simply how long participants are willing and able to spend away from their own place of employment (though in some cases this might be 'the longer, the better'!).

Many of these issues might also be related to when the event is scheduled to occur. In some senses this seems to require organizers to be somewhat omniscient, necessitating foresight of events twelve, eighteen or twenty-four months ahead. For example, many conferences already occupy 'traditional' slots in the academic calendar, meaning that organizing an event at this time will run the risk of limiting attendees who may choose to go elsewhere. Similarly, organizing an event during widely used teaching or examination/assessment periods of the academic calendar could also limit attendees (although again, it might appeal for lecture-weary academics!), as indeed could events organized during the main research (and/or holiday) periods of the academic calendar. Deliberations concerning when to schedule the event become even more complicated when the event is international in scope, as differences remain in academic calendars in different parts of the world. In short, and even before 'events' overtake events (train strikes, closures of roads, bad weather, and so on), event scheduling is probably much more restricted than would at first be imagined.

 # Venue location

The choice of venue is often a pragmatic decision, based on the location of the event organizers. However, where there is latitude to site a meeting elsewhere, or where options exist due to multiple organizers, consideration should be paid to transport access, facilities, cost, political message, and so on. For example, when the inaugural event of the International Critical Geography Group was organized in Vancouver, a certain amount of debate ensued on mailing lists regarding the costs involved and potential exclusion of postgraduates (and indeed undergraduates, interested others and so on) from what was perceived to be an unnecessarily expensive (and 'Western') choice of location. Mindful of such issues, the ICGG has located subsequent conferences more strategically, in South Korea (2000), Hungary (2002) and Mexico (2005). Another example is an annual, national postgraduate event (which one of us has co-organized for a number of years) that deliberately chooses a neutral (and inexpensive) venue, so that nobody is on home turf and everyone stays at the same venue (thus increasing social interaction).

 # Event format

The format is usually dictated by the kind of event being organized (for example, seminar, workshop, conference). In relation to conferences, the format is shaped by the extent to which the conference is open and inclusive, with all potential papers/presentations being accepted without review, or more restricted, perhaps based on the pre-review of submitted abstracts or even blind refereeing of pre-submitted papers (usually in the name of 'quality'). A further issue concerns how you want the event to 'run' – do you want it to be traditional/controlled, in the sense of paper-based presentations with limited potential for discussion, or more open and participatory/interactive? This might affect the types or number of rooms that are used for the event, from traditional tiered, fixed-furniture lecture theatres that make group-work rather difficult, to completely adaptable, (large) flat rooms where participants can adapt the surroundings to their own needs. It also links to the length of conference 'sessions' – how many papers do you want presented in each session? Experience suggests that a two-hour session is the limit before people need a break and refreshments.

For the largest-scale events, major international conferences with thousands of potential attendees, a range of other issues come to the fore (which you need to bear in mind if you work on the organizing committee of such an event – though they often have their own dedicated conference organizing staff).

- Large-scale meetings usually require venues and locations to be identified a number of years before the event actually occurs – the organizers may therefore have little room for manoeuvre as the event approaches and problems or issues arise.
- It is usually a case of identifying an area/city as the potential location, before beginning to identify the venue. However, identification of the former can be reliant on having a team of local volunteers who are willing to help organize the event, whereas the latter depends on the number of locations that actually meet the necessary criteria (number of rooms for accommodation, facilities for conference sessions and so on), and their respective costs – for the largest events the available range will be fairly limited.
- The facilities will need to have hundreds of sleeping rooms and as many meeting rooms as there are sessions, plus exhibition space to be accommodated.
- The range of potential venues will also be limited by the organizers' desire (or otherwise) to cater for the particular needs of the client group, and what those needs are (that is, the financial benefits that they can derive through the provision of services, such as provision of food, drink and so on).

● Participation/call for papers/publicity

Once most of the early key decisions have been taken (themes focused, dates identified, venues confirmed) it is then time to publicize the event so that potential attendees can be stimulated, and contributors identified.

Dependent on the style and format of the proposed event, you may wish to approach some potential ('keynote') speakers before this occurs, primarily to act as further incentive for people to attend and/or contribute. Incentives for such invited speakers vary, from monetary payment to forms of payment 'in kind' (such as waiving of event fees, payment of accommodation costs, and so on), but certainly it is best to avoid being held to ransom over the potential contribution of one or two speakers. A further incentive for people to contribute could be notification of either the intention to produce a post-event publication, or details of any pre-arranged agreement to publish selected works, or the entirety of presented material.

Event publicity information (perhaps disseminated via email discussion lists, via posters, flyers, and so on) should clearly state the key themes, the 'call for papers' (including how to submit a paper/submission, to whom, and by when), sponsor details (if applicable), invited speakers (see below), and where to access further information and relevant registration and bursary forms. The registration form should seek all the relevant information needed – name, address, affiliation, paper title, abstract, accommodation and catering requirements, and so on. It should clearly state costs, forms of payment and to whom payment should be made, and by what date the form should be returned (and any penalties associated with late payment). If possible an event website should be set up to house all this information, including forms for downloading – this can then be updated with the programme as the event draws near, including other details (or links) such as maps of the local area, details of local accommodation, food providers and so on.

 ## Accessibility and inclusivity

It should almost go without saying that meetings should be held in locations that *all* potential delegates can access, and not just in cost terms. This means ensuring that all the rooms used at the meeting are accessible to wheelchair users and people with mobility impairments; that there are accessible toilets nearby; that the accommodation available to delegates is fully accessible; and that if there is a long distance between meeting venues and accommodation that accessible transport is available. If a person uses a guide or mobility dog you should check to see whether the venue is happy to accommodate it and that the dog can travel to the venue easily (for example, Hawaii will not allow guide or mobility dogs to accompany their user without expensive tagging and quarantine; some countries do not allow the free passage of dogs).

Further, every endeavour should be made to make sessions and materials accessible. This means that if there are (partially) deaf delegates, signers are provided; if there are (partially) blind delegates, the programme is provided in Braille or on audio cassette and as large print, that the signage between rooms is also in large print, and that a large-print/tactile map of the meeting venue is provided; if there are wheelchair or mobility-impaired delegates, full access maps that detail the accessibility of buildings and the routes between them are provided (for a set of map symbols see http://www.nuim.ie/nirsa/mapsymbols.htm). Delegates should be strongly encouraged to have their talk on overheads as detailed bullet points, then those delegates who are (partially) deaf can still follow the talk.

In addition, helpers (such as wheelchair-pushers and guides) should be made available if required. Remember, the cost of travel for disabled delegates is often far higher than non-disabled delegates. This is especially the case if they have to travel with personal assistants. As good practice, you should not charge the personal assistant for attending the conference. Most of the measures detailed above are relatively cheap with the exception of signing. The simplest way to pay for it is to cross-subsidize from delegate fees. In practice, this will mean raising the fees modestly across all delegates.

 # Language

English is now often taken for granted as the universal language at international conferences, with little explicit resistance (see Kitchin, 2003/2005). For delegates whose first language is not English this can be highly problematic as it creates particular power relations that favour those for whom English is their native tongue. Native English-speakers can speak freely without having to perform on-the-spot translation. They can reply to questions without having to 'try to find' the right words. Further, those for whom English is not a first language often find it much easier to follow the written word rather than speech, where accents and speed of speech can make comprehension difficult.

All these issues need to be respected by both the conference organizers and delegates, with efforts made to provide as much material as possible in a written format and delegates encouraged to speak slowly, clearly and without slang or colloquialisms. One useful strategy to encourage among delegates is have their talk on overheads as detailed bullet points, then those delegates whose verbal English is poor but written English is good can still follow the presentation.

It should also be remembered that some delegates will have been on intensive language courses in order to attend the conference and will have spent months preparing an English language version of their talk. This effort should be respected. If members of the audience have questions these should be written down as well as spoken. Where possible there needs to be experimentation with translation. Professional interpreters are a potential solution, but they are extremely expensive and push conference costs up significantly, thus excluding those with limited budgets.

Customs and body language

Two aspects little considered by either meeting organizers or attendees are customs and body language. One of the most insidious aspects of many supposedly 'international' meetings is that because the lingua franca is English, native English-speakers also take it for granted that the social norms – in terms of social interaction, public behaviour, speaker–audience interaction, ways of asking questions, ways of addressing peers – of English-speaking societies are also the meeting's norm (see Kitchin, 2003/2005). This is clearly problematic for other delegates who can feel 'out-of-place' or obliged to adopt such norms. Moreover, it needs to be appreciated that body language varies from place to place, leaving some delegates unsure how to read gestures and react appropriately. Here, conference organizers need to encourage attendees to 'step outside' of their own traditions and to engage with new ways of knowing and doing. What might be useful in this respect is a workshop in good practice in communication/customs (for example, presentation, conduct, conference customs, body language) to be held at the start of each meeting.

Name-badge politics

As a meeting organizer you should be aware of what might be termed 'name-badge politics' – people being treated differently depending on their position of seniority or how well they are known to other delegates. There are no easy answers to this problem. Potential solutions might be to drop titles from name badges – so no 'Dr' or 'Prof' titles, to ensure mixing at social events and to ensure that postgraduate and junior faculty participate fully in sessions and events (for example, making sure there is a mix of experience on panels and so forth).

 ## Food and accommodation

Given the variety of people's eating habits, plus dietary conditions, you should endeavour to cater for all people's food preferences. This means providing menus that include vegetarian/vegan options, as well as catering for specific dietary needs. Alternatively it means providing no food at all at the event, but merely signposting attendees to sources of various types/budgets in the immediate vicinity. The same premise can apply to decisions over accommodation. It used to be the case that conference accommodation was either restricted to university halls of residence or a specific hotel. It is now increasingly common for delegates to be offered a preferred choice, but with a range of other options based on price and personal preference. Alternatively delegates can simply be offered details of all available local accommodation, allowing them to choose on the basis of taste, budget and so on.

 ## At the event

The smooth running of the actual event undoubtedly relates to the effectiveness of prior planning, but unforeseen circumstances or problems can arise which require prompt action. Such problems may take many forms, and often there is little that can be done by event organizers; however, many potential problems can be anticipated, and, cliché though it might be, the motto here is 'be prepared'. Perhaps the most obvious potential area of concern relates to the technical equipment being used during the event, and it is essential to have access to 'emergency' technical support should anything go wrong. Participants may also require access to email, printing services or photocopying provision, and so on. Box 21.1 provides a checklist of things to do just prior to the event and during its running.

Box 21.1 Conference checklist

Pre-arrangements
- If on a campus, advise security and agree security measures (e.g., when doors will be open/locked, etc.).
- Confirm appropriate exhibition material will be delivered and set up (e.g., podium, screens, projectors, display boards, etc.).
- Check if any pre-arranged parking arrangements are still in place.
- Check that accommodation and catering arrangements are still in place.
- Check conference facilities, including cloakroom and toilet facilities and heating arrangements.
- Liaise with media relations units and send appropriate publicity and press invites/releases one week ahead of the event.
- If needed, book a photographer to record a key event such as a plenary speech.
- Produce an evaluation form, if needed.
- Make sure that conference materials will be delivered on time and collated into suitable form (e.g., conference packs and name-badges prepared, evaluation form, etc.).
- Make sure there will be a supply of pens, paper, folders, etc.
- Make sure VIP/guest speakers are fully briefed one week in advance.
- Produce an attendance list.

Staffing
- Draw up a full schedule with all tasks indicated.
- Make sure that all tasks associated with the conference have someone assigned who knows their responsibilities (looking after rooms, VIPs, press, registration, etc.).
- If staff are to be paid, agree duties and payments in advance.
- Brief session chairs.

On the day(s)
- Arrive early and make sure all the equipment booked is where it is meant to be and is working, and that rooms are set up appropriately.

cont.

- Set up the reception desk and layout registration and conference materials.
- Set up any display material needed.
- Let the venue's central reception areas know where the event is being held.
- Make sure there is access to a phone.
- Ensure that there is adequate signage to and within the venue.
- Ensure the day's timetable is displayed outside each room being used.
- Make sure there is drinking water in each room and enough glasses.
- If there are VIP guests, make sure that someone is assigned to look after them (and that reserved seating is assigned and marked, accommodation booked, gifts sorted, etc.).
- Collect evaluation forms, if distributed.

 ## Social events

For many events it now seems as if the social activities and/or additional events (such as field trips, workshops and so on) are as big an enticement to attend as the dissemination of materials. For the event organizers, a wide range of options for pre-organized social activities/events and so on exist, each with different requirements of organizational endeavour. They range from the expensive to the free. For example, the 2004 Conference of the International Geographical Union (held in Glasgow, Scotland) offered participants the opportunity to visit Iceland with expert guides for an additional £1000 ($1500)! Alternatively, organizers might arrange a social evening in a local venue that might be just as pleasurable (and somewhat easier on the pocket). In many ways it is a case of 'judging your market' (your potential attendees) and making best use of what surrounds the event venue and location.

REFERENCES
Kitchin, R. (2003/2005) 'Cuestionando y destabilizando la hegemonia angloamericana y del inglés en geografia', *Documents d'Anàlisi Geogràfica* 42: 17-36, reprinted as 'Disrupting and destabilising Anglo-American and English-language hegemony in Geography', *Social and Cultural Geography*, 6(1): 1-7.

22 Final Words

In this book we have sought to make the practices, processes and politics of publishing academic research more transparent. In the main, we have tried to document the various forms of publication available to researchers, and how they work. Cleary many options are available, from writing articles for journals, drafting chapters for edited books, scripting a book, placing a note in a newsletter, talking to the media, presenting a paper at a conference, and so on. Further, each of these media have specific submission requirements, reach different audiences and have positives and negatives with regard to their perceived worth by university administrators. Between them, however, they provide a researcher with the capacity to communicate their work and ideas in whatever form and style they consider to be the most appropriate, permitting that work to be consumed by anyone, from an interested colleague to a handful of experts, from a local activist group to a large, global, lay audience.

Allied to this, we have sought to expose how academic publication is embedded in wider educational transformations. Publication is no longer simply about the communication of research and ideas; it is now an integral part of a wider business that is worth billions of dollars a year. Certainly, for those who can play the publication game, and play it well, there are now generous rewards on offer – increased salaries, preferential work conditions, support staffing, global mobility, relative fame and so on. Ultimately, however, these rewards are being generated at a price; an increasingly pressured work environment that does not necessarily serve research well.

Given the diversity of choices, set within the context of today's competitive, academic environment, it is increasingly vital that informed decisions are made about the best way to let others know about your findings and ideas. We have therefore argued that a strategic approach to publication is essential (whatever the rights or wrongs of the conditions that create such imperatives). Publishing academic endeavours needs to be tied to a specific goal or series of goals (whether that is securing a job or pro-motion, personal fulfilment, etc.); achieving this goal requires the identification of a suitable strategy and associated tactics and, in turn, these tactics need to be implemented. For us, the key to making this work, and for it to be fulfilling, is for the goal, strategy and tactics to be defined and con-trolled as much as possible by *you*. As such, we hope that our description of how various media operate, and how they are often valued by those that evaluate research outputs, helps you to assess the options available and successfully publicise your research.

In providing our advice we have tried not to fall into the trap of being overly prescriptive. There are no rules that, if followed, will definitely pro-duce successful results. Publication, like the rest of everyday life, is much more messy that that. However, by understanding how the various forms of publication work and how submissions are judged we hope we have shed some light on what might have first seemed impenetrable 'black boxes'.

While highlighting ways to survive and thrive within academia we have also tried to avoid the trap of seeming to endorse pernicious forms of research accountancy presently being used in higher education around the world. On the contrary, we hope our advice empowers you, rather than making you a slave to the system. Clearly other writers may well have approached the task of writing this book through a different set of experi-ences and alternative political viewpoints. Be that as it may, we hope that the practical advice we have offered here has been of use regardless of how you view the transformation of the higher education sector.

Finally, while we have detailed our own understandings of how vari-ous forms of publication work and how to approach them strategically, we would encourage you to seek out other expertises. In particular we are thinking here about your colleagues and peers along the corridors where you work and within your wider networks. These individuals have a ready supply of experiences and suggestions that you can draw upon to help you achieve your goals. Likewise, you can pass on your views to others no matter how humble they might be. As we stated in Chapter 1, there is no point in learning how the publication game works if no one else can learn and benefit from your observations and experiences.

Appendix 1 *USEFUL REFERENCES AND RESOURCES*

Tenure

NEA (2004) *The Truth About Tenure in Higher Education.*
http://www.nea.org/he/truth.html. Last accessed 4 August 2004.

Whicker, M.L., Jacobs Kronenfeld, J. and Strickland, R.A. (1993) *Getting Tenure.*
Newbury Park, CA: Sage.

General writing guides

Billingham, J. (2002) *Editing and Revising Text.* Oxford: Oxford University Press.

Booth, W.C., Colomb, G.G. and Williams, J.M. (2003) *The Craft of Research.* 2nd edn. Chicago: University of Chicago Press.

Luey, B. (2002) *Handbook for Academic Authors,* 4th edn. Cambridge: Cambridge University Press.

Palmer, R. (2002) *Write in Style: A Guide to Good English,* 2nd edn. London: Routledge.

Pearsall, T.E., Cunningham, D.H. and Smith, E.O. (2000) *How to Write for the World of Work,* 6th edn. Boston, MA: Heinle and Heinle.

Turabian, K.L. (1996) *A Manual for Writers,* 6th edn. Chicago: University of Chicago Press.

Williams, J.M. (2003) *Style: Ten Lessons in Clarity and Grace,* 7th edn. New York: Longman.

Grammar and punctuation

Stilman, A. (1997) *Grammatically Correct*. Cincinnati, OH: Writer's Digest Books.

Truss, L. (2003) *Eats, Shoots & Leaves: The Zero Tolerance Approach to Punctuation*. London: Profile Books.

Referencing

Chicago Manual of Style (1993) 14th edn. Chicago: University of Chicago Press, Chicago.

Map making

Robinson, A.H., Morrison, J.L, Muehrcke, P.C., Kimerling, A.J. and Guptil, S.C. (1995) *Elements of Cartography*, 5th edn. New York: John Wiley.

Plagiarism

Carroll, J. and Appleton, J. (2001) *Plagiarism: A Good Practice Guide*. Joint Information Systems Committee. Oxford: Oxford Brookes University.

Franklyn-Stokes, A. and Newstead, S.E. (1995) 'Undergraduate cheating: who does what and why', *Studies in Higher Education*, 20 (2): 159–72.

Copyright and intellectual property

Intellectual Property. http://www.intellectual-property.gov.uk/index.htm. Last accessed 4 August 2004.

World Intellectual Property Organization. http://www.wipo.int/. Last accessed 4 August 2004.

Report writing

Booth, P.F. (1991) *Report Writing*, 2nd edn. Huntingdon: Elm Publications.

Bowden, J. (2000) *Writing a Report*. Oxford: How To Books.

Williams, K (1995) *Writing Reports*. Oxford: The Oxford Centre for Staff Development.

Press releases

AlphaGalileo.
http://www.alphagalileo.org/index.cfm?fuseaction=ShowPage&pageid=14 Last accessed 4 August 2004.

Searchengines.com.
http://www.searchengines.com/marketing_free_press_release.html Last accessed 4 August 2004.

Writing for newspapers and magazines

Bagnall, N. (1993) *Newspaper Language*. Oxford: Focal Press.

Dick, J. (1996) *Writing for Magazines*. London: A&C Black.

Hicks, W., Adams, S. and Gilbert, H. (1999) *Writing for Journalists*. London: Routledge.

Jacobi, P.P. (1991) *The Magazine Article: How to Think It, Plan It, Write It*. Bloomington, IN: Indiana University Press.

Sloan Wray, C. (1997) *Writing for Magazines: A Beginner's Guide*. Lincolnwood, IL: NTC Publishing Group.

Book publishing

Clark, G. (1994) *Inside Book Publishing*, 2nd edn. London: Routledge.

Davies, G. (1995) *Book Commissioning and Acquisition*. London: Routledge.

Levine, M.L. (1988) *Negotiating a Book Contract*. Wakefield, RI: Moyer Bell.

Agents

Turner, B. (2004) *The Writers' Handbook*. London: Pan Books.

Self-publishing

Finch, P. (1997) *How to Publish Yourself.* London: Allison & Busby.

Poynter, D. (2003) *The Self-Publishing Manual: How to Write, Print and Sell Your Own Book.* London: Para Books.

Ross, T. and Ross, M. (2002) *The Complete Guide to Self-publishing: Everything You Need to Know to Write, Publish and Sell Your Own Book.* Cincinnati, OH: Writer's Digest Books.

Presenting

Billingham, J. (2003) *Giving Presentations.* Oxford: Oxford University Press.

Uncommon Knowledge http://www.uncommon-knowledge.co.uk/public_speaking.html. Last accessed 4 August 2004.

Networking

Fisher, D. and Vilas, S. (1996) *Successful Networking: The Key to Personal and Professional Success.* London: Thorsons.

Appendix 2 Questions Journal Editors Are Often Asked

For those unfamiliar with publishing journal articles the process can often seem a little unclear. To help you understand this process, we offer some answers to questions editors are often asked. This Appendix should be read in conjunction with Chapter 6, which provides general advice about writing articles and submitting them to journals.

What does an editor do?
An editor's job is to manage the day-to-day tasks in producing a journal – liaising with contributing authors, putting papers through the refereeing process, making decisions with regard to acceptance, allocating papers into issues, copyediting and making sure accepted papers are correctly formatted, and dealing with the publisher. In relation to liaising with authors, an editor's job is to balance trying to help an author publish an article at the same time as fulfilling the aims and objectives of the journal and maintaining the quality of the material published. To help in this task an editor relies on the guidance of an editorial board and referees. Most journals have more than one editor to help cope with the workload.

What is an editorial board and what does it do?
An editorial board is a panel of 'experts' chosen to help and guide the editor. Board members referee manuscripts and also advise the editor about the direction and quality of the journal and the identity of potential referees. How extensively the editor uses the editorial board varies across journals. It is the policy of some journals that every paper is refereed by at least one board member. Other journals use the board more selectively. Board members are chosen to provide expertise across the breadth of the journal's specialty. If the journal is international in scope, the board will seek to reflect this. Some journals have specific policies about selecting board members. For example, some seek to balance the gender of board members and/or blend seasoned academics with those at the start of their careers.

What is the role of a referee?

The referee's job is twofold. First, to guide the editor's decision as to whether the paper is worthy of publication. Second, to provide constructive advice to the author(s) so that they might improve the quality of their paper. (See Appendix 3.)

How are referees chosen?

Most papers address two or three inter-related themes so an editor will send a manuscript to two or more referees. Using their own knowledge and networks or drawing on the advice of board members, an editor will choose referees who have extensive knowledge of these themes. In general, editors will try to choose referees who do not have extensive links with the author(s). Some journals have specific policies concerning referee choice. For example, some journals stipulate that all three referees cannot be from the same continent. This is to ensure that the papers speak to an international audience.

Is the refereeing system anonymous?

Most journals operate a 'double blind' system of refereeing. That is, the author's identity is kept secret from the referees, and the referees' identity is secret from the author. Some journals are now encouraging referees to be more open in their refereeing by declaring their identity.

Can I have a say in the reviewers of my paper?

In general, it is the editor who chooses the referees. If, however, you have a particular reason for wanting to exclude a referee then write an explanatory note in the covering letter when you submit your paper.

How long should I have to wait for referee comments?

Journals vary in how long they give referees to provide a report, but the majority allow between one and three months. The waiting period can last longer than this though for various reasons. For example, a referee might not do the review, meaning that the editor has to find a replacement. Editors will try to keep you informed of the progress of your paper; if however you have not heard anything after four months send the editor an email or letter asking for an update.

Are manuscripts screened?

There are very few journals that adopt a policy of sending every article they receive out for review. Editors will screen the manuscripts and return papers that either do not fit the brief of the journal or are obviously below the standard expected (and will clearly not receive positive referees' reports in their present form).

Are articles by students treated differently?
No. Editors will treat every paper equally as long as it fits the brief of the journal and meets the required standard.

Will the journal accept an article that does not conform to the author guidelines?
Generally, an editor will ignore basic formatting until the final version, unless the paper is so badly formatted that it is unreadable. They are much more likely to balk at the length of an article. Editors have very strict rules given to them by the publishers concerning the number of pages in each issue. They therefore make strategic decisions about the length of articles they wish to publish, stating the desired length in the 'notes for authors' (e.g. 'articles should be no more than 7000 words including references'). If an article far exceeds the desired word length, it is likely that it will be returned for revisions. (See Chapter 6.)

Will the journal publish colour plates?
Printing colour is very expensive and most journals will not publish colour plates. Those journals that will print in colour often require a justification as to why the plate should be in colour and not black and white.

Is it possible to include non-standard media with the publication, e.g. a CD?
It is highly unlikely that a journal will accept non-standard media (e.g. not a word-processed or image file) for distribution with your article. This is for reasons of cost, production, distribution, and cataloguing. There are also licensing, copyright and security issues about distributing software and data. The easiest solution is perhaps to provide details of where a reader can obtain a copy of the data (e.g. asking them to contact you directly or provide a web link). If you feel it is essential that the CD or other medium is distributed with your article, contact the journal editor or publisher and discuss whether they are prepared to work with you.

How do I go about proposing special sections/issues or offering to write a commentary/editorial?
Editors are always on the lookout for quality submissions. If you have organized a conference and feel that the papers would make a coherent collection, or if you have an idea for a commentary or editorial, then simply contact the editor with your proposal. The editor will assess your proposal and if interested will accept it as is, or work with you to develop it. Papers submitted as part of a special section/issue will go through the same refereeing process as other papers.

What is the journal's acceptance rate?
You should realize that *all* journals reject some articles. The acceptance rate is the percentage of articles submitted that are accepted for publication. The

acceptance rate varies across journals depending on the standard they are seeking. The most respected and high profile journals tend to have lower acceptance rates than other journals simply because they have the most submissions and space is limited. It is important to note that the acceptance rate is not always a measure of how hard it is to get an article published, but rather reflects the quality of the papers submitted. No journal aims to reject a certain percentage and editors will accept all papers that reach a certain standard (which of course can be very high in some cases). In many ways the acceptance rate is immaterial. If your article is of a high quality it will be accepted and published. If you still want to know the rate, some journals publish them; otherwise contact the editor.

What is the journal's citation index score/rating?

A citation index reveals the extent to which articles within a journal are cited in other articles. The higher the citation index the more often articles in that journal are cited. ISI, a private company, calculates the academic standard citation index scores. These scores are available through subscription for a product entitled 'Web of Knowledge'. Some caution needs to be used when considering the index. For example, new journals do not get a rating for a number of years, but it does not mean that they are not well read. Also the index does not necessarily mean that your intended readership will read your paper.

What is the circulation/size of readership of the journal?

Journal subscriptions consist of three types: individual, institutional (library), and online through package deals (for example, *Science Direct, SwetsWise,* etc. provides online access to hundreds of journals). It is therefore increasingly difficult to track the circulation of a journal, and next to impossible to know the size of readership. This is especially the case given the widespread use of electronic databases such as *FirstSearch* that allow potential articles of interest to be identified without having to browse through each issue. That said, some journals *are* clearly more read than others – reputation and the citation index rating probably best reflect this.

Is this a good journal to choose in terms of my tenure/RAE?

It is up to you to make this decision in consultation with your own institution. Some editors will also give you their personal opinions if asked. Another indicator might be to consider the journal's ISI citation index, if it has one. This index has become, rightly or wrongly, a surrogate indicator of a journal's academic worth as it provides a measure of the extent to which a journal is read and its articles cited.

Can I challenge the editor's decision?

Yes. If you feel that you have been hard done by then you do have the right to ask an editor to reconsider their decision. You will need to detail the reasons as to why you think a decision should be changed.

Do I get paid for my contribution?
In general, authors do not get paid for contributing articles to academic journals. If you are looking to earn money from publishing academic work some of the popular press magazines pay for contributions, as do newspapers.

How long will it take for my article to be published?
Once the article has been accepted for publication it will go into the queue for publication. How long it takes until actual publication depends on how long the queue is. For some journals this will mean you will go straight into the next issue and for others you may wait two years or more. Generally, new journals will have shorter queues than the more established and top-ranking journals, but this is highly variable.

Who holds the copyright, the author or the publisher?
It is almost standard that the publisher of a journal will hold the copyright for the article once it is published. However, authors can reproduce their own article elsewhere provided that full acknowledgement is given to the journal as the original source of publication and that the publisher is informed so they know there has not been a breach of copyright (see Chapter 5)

How many offprints will I receive?
An offprint is a reproduction of an article. The number an author receives depends on the policy of the journal. Most academic journals will provide in the region of twenty-five offprints free of charge. Some journals now provide the offprint as a .pdf file.

Appendix 3 *REFEREEING FOR JOURNALS, PUBLISHERS AND CONFERENCES*

Although not a task undertaken in relation to publishing your own research, we have included an appendix on refereeing because it is an integral aspect of the publication process. All articles submitted to refereed journals are peer-reviewed, 'experts' employed by the publishers vet most book proposals, and a number of conferences now review potential papers before selecting which will go into the programme.

The role of a referee is . . .

- To help the editor make a decision as to whether the paper is worthy of publication
- To provide constructive advice to the author(s) so that they might improve the quality of their paper.

A referee should be . . .

Constructive, helpful and insightful
As noted above, one of the primary roles of a referee is to help the author(s) improve their paper. Constructive criticism, helpful hints and insightful comments provide authors with valuable guidance as to how they might address any perceived shortcomings of their work.

Respectful of the right to different ideas
A referee's job is to assess the scholarship of a paper, not to police the ideas that are presented. This means being respectful of differing viewpoints, and yet still being critical of their coherence. In other words, the arguments made should be evaluated on their respective merits, and not simply dismissed as 'wrong' or 'out-of-date'.

Mindful of their position as a 'gatekeeper'

Referees are gatekeepers to publications, and with this position comes a *responsibility* to be fair to the author. It is important to remember that the author(s) will have spent several months to years undertaking their attempt at publishing. Ill-phrased and dismissive refereeing could unnecessarily knock their confidence and ruin what should be a fulfilling exercise.

Aware and respectful of deadlines

Editors are aware that they are reliant on professional courtesy for reviews by referees. That said, the editor also has to manage the journal in a timely manner and to provide comments to the author within a certain time frame (normally two to three months). Editors are therefore reliant on referees to honour the commitment they gave when they agreed to review the paper. As an author, a referee would expect their own article be reviewed to schedule; as a referee, they should respect the expectations of others.

A referee should never . . .

Be patronizing, condescending or malicious

There is no justification for writing a deliberately destructive referee's report that is patronizing, condescending or malicious. A referee can recommend rejection for good reasons and still be kind to the author. If a referee feels that they cannot write this kind of report, they should return the paper to the editor and let someone who will be more constructive undertake the report. One point to remember is that English is spoken by only 8 per cent of the world population.

Be personal

A referee's report should never be a personal attack against an individual (with comments such as 'this person is an idiot'). Evaluation should be based solely on the merit or ideas contained in the paper, and not on who wrote it.

Be over-particular

The role of the referee is not to try to find all the faults in the paper but to give an overall assessment. Moreover, if the author can address the shortcomings of the paper with reasonable effort, the referee should not over-emphasize the faults but then recommend publication with only minor revisions.

Be self-promoting

The referee's report is a constructive assessment of the paper under review, not an opportunity for the referee to promote their opinion at the expense of the authors. The report should also not be used as an opportunity to force the author to cite the referee's work if it is only tangentially related to theirs.

Be reactive

Undertaking and writing-up research is all about critiquing and developing ideas. Therefore a referee should not overreact to arguments that criticize their previous contributions. Instead, the arguments should be evaluated on their own merits.

Express favouritism

The refereeing process is designed to ensure that quality articles are published. There is therefore a responsibility on the referee to be impartial and to help the editor make a decision. Each article should be judged on its merits and should not be tainted by favouritism, whereby a paper that supports the referee's own position, or is written by a colleague, is given support when it does not deserve it. Such favouritism does not aid the author, whereas constructive criticism would have helped to improve the article's quality.

Plagiarize the ideas in the paper

Even though the paper has not yet been published, the ideas expressed within it are the intellectual property of the author. If a referee feels the idea is of sufficient merit to use it themselves or it inspires them to write a related paper they should recommend publication, even if the paper is badly written (this can always be addressed), and ask the editor when the paper will be published so that they can cite it.

Circulate or cite the paper without the permission of the author

The version of the paper submitted to the journal is an initial draft and it is sent to a referee for evaluation in confidence that this version will not be circulated to colleagues or cited without permission.

Writing a referee's report

There are three basic rules to writing a referee's report.

1 Follow the guidelines as set out by the journal editor. Every journal has a different set of aims and objectives. As a consequence, while each editor is looking for good quality contributions, each will have particular criteria by which they would like the paper to be judged. These criteria will accompany the paper.
2 Always start and end on a positive note even if you think a paper does not merit publication in its present form.
3 Follow the recommendations regarding referee conduct as set out above.

In general, a referee's report will consist of two sections: a covering letter and a summary report.

The covering letter

The letter need not be long, as the substantive discussion of the paper will be in the report. However, it should include the manuscript number and title along with the overall recommendation: accept as is, accept with revisions, revise and resubmit, reject (see Chapter 6).

The summary report

The summary report most often consists of two sections. The first will be a checklist supplied by the editor. This will simply require the referee to check boxes or rate the paper against a set of criteria. The second section will be an open-ended report discussing the merits and faults of the paper, along with general suggestions for improving the paper including advice about the argument made or structure of the paper, and for additional work that might be required. This discussion might be guided by questions from the editor, such as those outlined on page 45.

It is helpful to both editor and author if those things that the referee judges *must* be done before publication are distinguished clearly from those that *might* be done. As far as possible, a negative review should explain to the authors the weaknesses of their manuscript, so that rejected authors can understand the basis for the decision.

Some journals will ask for a report that will be sent to the author, and a shorter report that will be seen only by the editor.

Common questions concerning refereeing

Are referees compensated in any way?

In general, no. Editors rely on professional courtesy given that the referees themselves are reliant on others to referee their papers when they submit them to a journal. Recently, some publishers have started to reward referees with discount vouchers on their products. Editorial board members will receive a free subscription to the journal for the period they serve on the board.

When can I reasonably decline a request to referee a paper?

If you are asked to referee a paper there is no obligation that you undertake this task. However, given professional courtesy and the fact that anyone who wants to publish an article is similarly reliant on referees, it is generally expected that referees will review a paper unless there is a particular reason that means that they cannot undertake the task. Such reasons might be a conflict of interest or an over-familiarity with the author and their work that hinders fair and 'objective' comment, or that the paper concerns a topic on which the referee feels unqualified to pass 'expert' comment. It should be noted that some journals may have penalties for refusal, such as barring the referee from submitting to that journal for a couple of years. If you must decline, let the editor know quickly (within a few days of receiving the paper), by fax or e-mail. Some journals will want you to return the paper so that it can be sent out again. Others will simply photocopy the one on file. If you do decline to review a paper it is always helpful to the editor if you provide the names and addresses of alternative referees.

How much time should I spend refereeing a paper?
This often depends on the article being read. A paper that is very well written and is almost publishable 'as is' takes less time to review because it takes less time to read and there are fewer comments to write. Similarly, a paper that is extremely poorly written with weak argument may not take long to review because it clearly is not going to get through the publication process, despite constructive criticism. Papers that display potential but are not yet of the required standard generally take the longest time to referee. This is because they require detailed reports that suggest ways to improve the paper. Experience tells us that a good, constructive review will take up to three to four hours to complete.

How long should a referee's report be?
There is no set length for a report, however it should be of a sufficient length that it explains fully to the editor and the author the reasoning behind a decision and ways to improve the paper to the required standard. This generally means that the review will have some substantive content. A report that consists of one or two sentences but recommends rejection or major revisions is of little help. The basic rule is to produce a report that you yourself would appreciate receiving.

Will I get to see what the other referees recommended?
This depends on the journal. Some journals have recently adopted a policy whereby all the referees' reports are sent to all the referees of a paper so that they know how their assessment compared to that of others.

Are referees' reports edited or censored by the journal editor?
Generally no, but they can be, especially if a report is unhelpful, malicious or offensive.

What should I do if I have already refereed the paper for another journal?
Inform the editor straight away. They will make a decision as to how to proceed. There might be very good reasons as to why the paper was resubmitted to the new journal. For example, the first journal might have felt that the paper was inappropriate and was more suited to the aims and objectives of the current journal. Further, the author may have felt unfairly treated or misunderstood by the first journal.

How does one become a referee?
Generally one gets selected to review papers by becoming known to the editor or an editorial board member as an expert in a particular field. So the more you publish or present work at conferences, the more likely you are to be asked to referee papers related to your topic of interest.

What if I want to get in contact with the author of the paper?
If you wish to be put in contact with the author of the paper most editors will be happy to act as a go-between, making sure each party is happy to be identified before releasing contact details.

Index